Management Practices of Successful CEOs

Memoir of a Psychological Consultant to Management

Management Practices of Successful CEOs

Memoir of a Psychological Consultant to Management

James P. Armatas, Ph.D.

Management Practices of Successful CEOs:
Memoir of a Psychological Consultant to Management
© 2020, James P. Armatas. All rights reserved.

Published by Desert Haven Publishing Company
La Quinta, CA

ISBN 978-1-7346414-0-0 (paperback)
ISBN 978-1-7346414-2-4 (hardcover)
ISBN 978-1-7346414-1-7 (eBook)
Library of Congress Control Number: 2020904328

DEDICATION

In appreciation for Rena J. Armatas, my wife of sixty-three years, for her loyalty, support and perceptive observations.

CONTENTS

PREFACE

At the writing of this introduction, I am eighty-seven years old and retired from a career as a psychological consultant to management. Over the past two years, three of the elder CEOs with whom I consulted died, leading me to reflect about them and what I learned from them. Each was a true entrepreneur who started or acquired a start-up business. Each achieved significant success, and each had unique management talents, skills, and experiences worthy of a major case study.

- Del Dunmire died in 2016 at the age of eighty-two. A convicted bank robber turned entrepreneur, Dunmire assembled incredible wealth through Growth Industries, a small start-up company that created sales and product monopolies manufacturing aircraft parts.

- Garry Drummond died in 2016 at the age of seventy-eight as the richest man in Alabama. Drummond grew a small Drummond Company into one of the largest coal companies in the world.

- Dave Noble, who died in 2017 at the age of eighty-five, parlayed a small financed insurance company with twelve employees into the American Equity Investment Life Insurance Company, a leading annuity insurer listed on the New York Stock Exchange.

My enthusiasm for these three leaders notwithstanding, I realized that during my career, I have learned much about management from all CEOs with whom I have been associated. This memoir is a tribute to the client companies and CEOs that I served over my career as a management consultant.

They include large and small companies that cut across the history of American industry from multilayered monopolies to a single-person enterprise. With few exceptions, all companies were survivors. They are still in business today, or they have merged with other companies at a substantial profit.

In an essay first published in 1958, Peter Drucker, the father of management theory, describes the five conditions essential for the survival of any enterprise:[1]

1. To Drucker, an organization is an assemblage of individuals working for a common event that must survive the lifespan of any one person. Most management decisions do not have a short-term impact for at least five years, and it might take ten or fifteen years to determine their longer-term effectiveness.
2. A business enterprise does not live in a vacuum. Society and/or economy can put any business out of existence overnight—nothing is simpler.
3. The only reason for existence of a business is that it has found a way to provide goods and services economically and efficiently.
4. To survive, a company must strive to become an innovator of change.
5. The absolute requirement of survival, for Drucker, is profitability, with a minimum that will most likely exceed the maximum toward which the company is striving.

Over these past fifty years, American business and industry have gone through significant transformational change. From a strong base of large monopolistic organizations and manufacturers providing career employment and benefits to prospective managers, the present culture opens career opportunities for resourceful CEOs and entrepreneurs.

I view this memoir not unlike a longitudinal research project, identifying the management practices of successful CEOs and their companies as models for a new generation of entrepreneurs and future CEOs to consider.

J.P.A.

INTRODUCTION

A lthough psychological consultants to management can become involved with numerous functions, the primary introduction is for assessment of both external and internal candidates. In the early twentieth century, psychology was identified closely with the development of intelligence testing. A test, as defined by Lee Cronbach, "is a systematic procedure for comparing the behaviors of two or more persons," and research in both Europe and America led to the introduction of tests of intelligence and tests measuring abilities to perform specific tasks.[2] World War I provided rapid development of intelligence test applications in standardizing procedures and in establishing norms and statistical applications in both Allied and Axis armies.

The intelligence test has become a commonplace assessment tool in educational, industrial, military, and clinical settings. Beyond obtaining a simple numerical IQ value, however, psychologists broaden their scope of assessment to understand an individual's cognitive processes, such as determining how the individual solves problems and identifying those factors that may be interfering with adaptive thinking.

Beyond intelligence assessment, personality assessment is an equally important or even greater expectation of the tasks expected of a psychologist. Whereas most psychologists might agree that the best way to measure intelligence is through an intelligence test, there is no such agreement on how to assess personality. Two philosophies have emerged, as depicted by Gordon Allport—one with methodologies based on group norms (nomothetic), and the other based on individualized data (idiographic)[3] and by Paul Meehl's distinction between clinical and actuarial prediction.[4]

Psychologists, obviously, have always found out about people by talking with them, so the interview has emerged as a primary source of information. Starting as an unstructured conversation, the interview evolved into a structured focus on areas determined to have relevance in understanding a person's present and future behavior. Patterned interviews became commonplace in the 1940s, consisting of standard questions determined to be relevant. Consistent with Meehl's dichotomy, some psychologists placed more faith in actuarial rather than interview conclusions.

Since World War II, the evolution of psychology has been dramatic. The field of clinical psychology was "born" in 1949 at the Boulder conference at the University of Colorado. In a massive undertaking to serve veterans, the Veterans Administration (VA), in collaboration with the American Psychological Association, established training programs in clinical/counseling psychology at selected major universities to provide four-year programs leading to Ph.D. degrees for students selected as VA psychology trainees.

In addition to university studies, a trainee spent a total of 4,000 hours over four years receiving on-the-job training in providing services to veterans in VA medical facilities. Individual psychology services were staffed with professors from participating universities, until the positions could be filled by graduates of the training programs. Initially, over 90 percent of clinical psychologists in America were trained by the VA.

Another dramatic psychological development was attributed to Kurt Lewin, recognized as the founder of modern social psychology and a pioneer in the field of action research, group dynamics, and organizational psychology. He became the founder of the National Training Laboratory (NTL), known for introducing Training Group (T-Group) management development experiences.

The Genesis of Psychological Consulting to Management

The creation of a practice called psychological consulting to management is attributed primarily to one man: Perry L. Rohrer. While serving as a psychologist in the military during World War II, Rohrer is reputed to have created a unique niche as an adviser to higher-level military officers confronted with issues related to the selection and development of their individual officer staffs. Following his discharge in 1945, he established the firm of Rohrer, Hibler & Replogle (RH&R), psychological consultants to management in Chicago, with branch offices in many of the major cities in the United States. RH&R is still active today, having expanded internationally to most of the major industrial cities.

I believe that the success of RH&R and other practitioners, such as myself, are related directly to the creative genius of Perry Rohrer. He firmly believed that a psychologist could make a valuable contribution to the development of individual managers, which in turn enhances the development of the organization. He also recognized the talents of psychologists had to be sold.

His model was simple. He approached successful, enlightened companies willing to spend consulting dollars on the personal development of existing and promising future executives.

Rohrer required the CEO of the organization to undertake a psychological assessment, which would be followed by an assessment report and a feedback session with the assessor. The CEO then had the option of inviting his or her key executives to undergo the assessment procedure with the understanding that the opportunity was voluntary, that the interview was confidential, and that the written report was maintained in a private file by the CEO. If the executive staff concurred, a schedule was set to include other executives and promising the same understanding that assessments were voluntary and confidential, and the written reports were guarded closely.

In going forward, no contracts were signed. It was understood that a consulting visit was a full day. In addition to scheduling assessment and feedback sessions, the psychologist had time for a range of consulting assignments at the discretion of individual managers. A monthly schedule was established with the understanding that the client could terminate the relationship at any time. Relationships usually lasted for years.

Most of the individuals joining RH&R did not have experience in business. In fact, some were not even psychologists. They were academicians—either teachers or administrators. What they did have in common were Ph.D. degrees, a professional presence, and superior articulation skills. Rohrer seemed to select candidates with sales skills in addition to professional credentials.

Rohrer created a patterned interview procedure touching on intellectual characteristics, emotional characteristics, motivational characteristics, insight into self and others, and interpersonal characteristics. Rohrer believed that what a person did in the past is the best predictor of what he or she would do in the future. The patterned interview used by many RH&R associates consisted of questions concerning a person's past experiences.

Background of Training

With a master's degree in public service from the University of Colorado that included a practicum working with delinquent boys, I accepted a position in January of 1955 as assistant dean at an Episcopal home for delinquent boys in Salina, Kansas. Our consulting clinical psychologist from the University of Kansas enlightened me that the VA psychology training program at the University of Kansas was one of the top programs in the country, providing diverse training in three different medical centers—including the VA's top psychiatric center. I started working for my Ph.D. in psychology at the University of Kansas in September of 1955 as a VA trainee.

I completed all requirements for a degree, including a full-year internship at the VA Center in Leavenworth, Kansas, in December 1958. Prior to completing my degree, a serendipitous experience altered my career direction. My wife's ex-roommate in Kansas City had accepted a position as secretary to Ralph Ogan and Harvey Thomas, psychological consultants to management in the firm of Ogan, Thomas & Associates.

Ralph was an original member of RH&R and headed the Kansas City office. In its corporate evolution, RH&R suffered some major realignments. In response to an ultimatum that all staff sign loyalty oaths, most of the staff, including Ralph Ogan, resigned. Overnight, RH&R offices became independently owned and operated, and bonded loosely through friendships.

Following my graduation, I was offered two jobs: one as a clinical/ counseling psychologist at the VA Center in Leavenworth, Kansas, and the other—through the connection of my wife's friend—as a staff psychologist with Ogan, Thomas. With the demand for clinical psychologists in the VA, I negotiated a part-time position with the VA, freeing me to do part-time consulting with Ogan, Thomas. Both Ralph and Harvey were gracious in providing training, client assignments, and freedom to develop my own methodologies, but I recognized my career limitations as an associate.

After approximately five years, I formed my own consulting organization, James P. Armatas & Associates, Inc. I enjoyed both of my careers. I stayed with my VA career for twenty years, but ultimately gave up my VA career as my consulting practice grew.

I hated to give up the VA. It gave me a firsthand perspective on the effect of the environment on behavior. The Leavenworth VA Center was a large extended care facility for veterans with chronic disabilities. It consisted of a general medical and surgical hospital with 300 beds and a nursing home with 120 beds, a psychiatric hospital with 250 beds, and a domiciliary (once referred to as an old soldier's home) with 1,000 beds.

Unlike training hospitals allied with major university medical centers, extended care facilities were bastions of custodial care resulting in chronic institutionalization. Two-thirds of domiciliary members had histories of alcoholism or mental illness. The psychiatric hospital was a page out of *One Flew Over the Cuckoo's Nest*.

As a board certified clinical psychologist in an understaffed center, a primary concern was in challenging the bureaucracies, working with nurses and support staff to teach and encourage the staff to learn ways of enlarging daily experiences in the lives of patients and members. A significant element of my work at Leavenworth involved a four-year research and demonstration grant I received from the Department of Health, Education and Welfare for a special residential and community training program for chronically institutionalized patients.[5]

Business was totally alien to me, but as my mentor, Harvey Thomas, explained, my clients would train me. In as much as a large part of an interview involved the workplace, I looked forward to my learning from the person I was interviewing as much as he/she was anticipating my assessment feedback.

At the same time, I used my skills and training as a clinical psychologist to make sure that my assessment and feedback sessions were relevant and insightful to the client. Well-trained clinicians no longer could be categorized as following simplistic nomothetic or idiographic method-ologies, but rather they followed a researcher/practitioner model using actuarial tools as one part in a research armamentarium.

Other skills I brought to my career in consulting to management came from my training in group dynamics and organizational development. A favorite tool I used throughout my career, attributed to Kurt Lewin, was action research, which involved attacking a problem quickly with empirical and interview data presented to management, resulting in immediate action strategies to address the problem. Although I didn't know management, I knew a strategy for solving problems.

The Assessment Procedure

Although I interviewed and wrote assessment reports on candidates for employment, most of my assessments were for management development with existing company management staff. Both groups obviously were generally regarded as capable individuals. The external candidates were either provided by a search firm or had been recommended by the company human resources assessors.

The assessment consisted of a confidential interview and psychological testing that included selections of intellectual and problem-solving tasks and select personality and projective tests.

Following each assessment, I wrote a report that was usually presented to the CEO. I subsequently scheduled individual developmental feedback sessions with the internal staff and external candidates who had been hired.

To me, the feedback session was by far the most critical part of the assessment procedure. My presence in the company was predicated on making managers more effective. The feedback was my opportunity to provide meaningful feedback to candidates, but more importantly, it was my opportunity to bond a relationship with a client not too different from that of an action research therapist/client relationship.

I typically interviewed a population of ambitious, highly competitive people. Drawing on Interpersonal Theory concepts,[6] my feedback sessions often addressed issues of dominance and submission. Helping young executives to understand the effects of their behavior in seeking to reach their goals, was one of the most rewarding aspects of my practice.

Format

Consistent with Perry Rohrer's model, my client companies were successful, enlightened and willing to spend consulting dollars on the personal development of existing and promising future executives. The following vignettes describe how they achieved their status and how their future unfolded. The vignettes include chapters on the three entrepreneurs (Del Dunmire, Garry Drummond, and Dave Noble), conglomerates (ITT/Colt Industries), multidivisional companies, legal monopolies, service companies, restaurants, and manufacturing companies.

In putting this memoir into perspective, I list client companies ranging from International Telephone & Telegraph Corporation (ITT) with 300 companies and 375,000 employees to Coalter Investments, a consulting manager of failing companies with one employer. In between are other multidivisional and large public companies but also individual, privately owned companies and the various roles of CEOs, executives and entrepreneurs with whom I consulted.

In addition to describing my personal experiences, I attempt to present the management practices and models of successful CEOs and companies in the various industries.

As a memoir, most of the content reflects my memory. In areas in which I reference documents, I try to identify the source. In commentary about the histories of companies before and beyond my tenure, I resort primarily to unreferenced online newspaper accounts or to Wikipedia.

CHAPTER ONE

THREE ENTREPRENEURS

In analyzing the group of companies selected for this memoir, I consulted with some companies for extended periods of ten to forty years. My contributions with other companies can be measured in months. Recognizing the vast variability in my knowledge and experience with client companies, I decided to set priorities in my presentations.

I had long, extensive consulting relationships with the three CEOs in whose memory I started this memoir (Del Dunmire, Growth Industries; Garry Drummond, the Drummond Company; and Dave Noble, American Equity Investment Life). All were successful entrepreneurs, resulting in my writing an in-depth vignette for each company. Their differences were obvious in the markets they served, but I also discovered that as successful entrepreneurs, they had similar management styles and practices.

This chapter contains the individual vignettes of the three CEOs, comments about their unique attributes, and a working model that combines these attributes as guidelines for managers and aspiring entrepreneurs.

Delbert L. Dunmire, Growth Industries

Without question, Delbert (Del) Dunmire is one of the most interesting, successful, and unique entrepreneurs I ever knew. He is from a breed of highly successful but controversial individuals who somehow was endowed with and/or acquired an uncanny ability to attain success, wealth, and power.

Approximately fifteen years ago, I collaborated with Dunmire on a book, interviewing him about his management philosophies and practices. The book was never published. His style never changed, and parts of this vignette are pulled from the original manuscript.

Dunmire was raised in Punxsutawney, Pennsylvania, and as a child would walk along railroad tracks looking for coal to heat the family home that was rented for $5 per month. He completed three years in engineering at the University of Buffalo by working as a machinist, then joined the Air Force.

Del Dunmire was known as the bank robber who became a millionaire. As an Air Force navigator and officer with a wife and child, he robbed a bank in Abilene, Kansas, to pay off a gambling debt. He was subsequently caught and ended up serving two years in the Kansas State Prison.

With skill as a machinist, he set up a shop in his garage in Grandview, Missouri, which led to Growth Industries, a firm providing aftermarket aircraft parts to airlines. His only business training was through two books he studied in prison, *The Prince* by Niccolò Machiavelli and *How to Win Friends and Influence People* by Dale Carnegie.

After struggling for several years, he learned through experience that mass production at a competitive price was a ticket to oblivion, while creating one aircraft part for one airline could lead to the fabulous wealth of a monopoly. Through his unique leadership talents, Dunmire developed state-of-the-art production and sales/marketing operations that served as a base for his success that started with one job with Trans World Airlines, better known as TWA.

My first contact with Dunmire was about fifteen years after he started Growth Industries. He had hired Bud Burgess, from Business Men's Assurance Company (BMA), one of my best clients, to head human resources. Burgess had mentioned my name and what I did at BMA, and Dunmire wanted to meet me. At our first meeting, Dunmire had me assess him and subsequently gave me carte blanche to spend whatever time I wanted at the company. My recommendation was for me to have a limited monthly schedule spread over a longer period. When I explained my fee, Dunmire said that was not enough. He said that Burgess said I was the best in town. He then said his advisers were the best available and that he insisted on paying them top dollar. I did not argue.

In 1979, while the company was going through a Chapter 11 bankruptcy, his brief bank robbing exploits made headlines in the Kansas City–area newspapers. The bankruptcy was short, and his company achieved phenomenal profitability through the years. The public also became more aware of his success as a business leader, public figure, and philanthropist.

"Some of the most important things you will learn at Growth Industries will be about yourself," Del Dunmire said to new employees. Dunmire believed strongly that the road to success entailed hiring the right people and maintaining a close, developmental relationship with them. According to Dunmire,

I'm concerned with developing my people. I like to think that I expect more of an employee than he will expect of himself. I sincerely feel the thing each person learns at Growth Industries is about him or herself. I feel that to grow, a person needs to have feedback about performance, both positive and negative.

Dunmire was a keen observer of behavior and a natural raconteur. As a consultant, I feel I made a professional contribution to Growth Industries. In return, in addition to the fee I collected, Dunmire spent untold hours helping me understand what I did not know about the business and management side of running my own consulting practice.

Dunmire's exploits were legion and often audacious. When he married for the second time, in 1986, he had a $1 million wedding in Kansas City, complete with marching band, movie stars, and total command of one of the largest hotels in Kansas City. The guest list? Simply 1,000 of his friends, associates, and would-be friends and associates from Kansas City and around the world. When the incumbent mayor of Kansas City refused to support a drug enforcement program, Dunmire provided $300,000 to the campaign of his opponent, who endorsed the program. At the thirtieth reunion of his high school graduating class in Punxsutawney, Dunmire took all the graduates and their spouses and guests—a total of over 450 people—on an excursion to the Bahamas at a cost of $500,000.

To balance the picture of extravagance, Dunmire was one of the largest individual contributors to charities in Kansas City. He gave hundreds of thousands of dollars each year. When a drive to build a Vietnam veterans memorial fell short by $150,000, Dunmire made up the shortfall. He personally endowed a civic board to fight drug use in Missouri.

The drug containment/rehabilitation program in his manufacturing company received national recognition by NBC television.

A human-interest story on Dunmire, which projected him into the national limelight, involved his return to the scene of his bank robbery in Abilene. He donated $50,000 to the city to build a band shell, while also distributing a grab bag filled with $45,000 in cash that was shared by all of those attending the contribution ceremony. Oh, by the way, while he was in Abilene, Dunmire also bought the bank building that he robbed!

Dunmire's exploits unquestionably are outlandish, but his business acumen was impressive. Very few managers or potential managers could— or would—run a company exactly like Del Dunmire. His individuality and intensity permeated Growth Industries and left a distinctive mark difficult for any one person to emulate. On the other hand, every manager or entrepreneur can learn something useful from Del Dunmire. He spent his life experimenting with his own company, developing management strategies that were successful and enormously profitable for him.

Dunmire's flamboyance and spending habits belied a very conservative approach to fiscal management. His spending was strategic and designed to help him increase his wealth. His manufacturing facility was filled with state-of-the-art equipment, but it was run with minimal expense. With his vast holdings, he was not leveraged. He had no debt. Before he invested in anything, he carefully evaluated his downside risk. He was a contrarian. He invested when things were out of favor, and he would not chase anything hyped beyond its value. He remembered lean times and time spent working his way out of bankruptcy.

His primary business strategy was survival. The key to his management success was that he never strayed from what he felt were the most basic elements of business. Through his own resourcefulness, he became an expert in the esoteric area known as entrepreneurial management.

Dunmire attributed his success to three principal ingredients that had little relation to any formal management skills:

1. Quality and knowledge of the product. He continued to upgrade his technical edge by investing in skilled workers and advanced equipment to make sure the product would be in demand.
2. Pricing. A prime contractor always commands a top price. Dunmire felt that with high quality and advanced technology he could command a high price.
3. Markets, the customers you serve. No matter what the quality of the product and regardless of whether the customer accepts the price, if the customer does not need the product or cannot pay the price, the enterprise cannot succeed.

As the business grew through the 1960s and early 1970s, the company prospered. By producing a precision product, Growth performed subcontract work for prime aerospace contractors with lucrative contracts that were able to pay top dollar for quality work. Dunmire, in turn, reinvested earnings into the most up-to-date machine tools, further enhancing his reputation as a high-technology subcontractor.

Life in those days was satisfying. And then the recession of 1972–1974 hit. Almost 100 percent of the business of Growth Industries came from government contracts. The contracts dried up and the backlog was nonexistent. Dunmire became aware of his company's vulnerability and its desperate need to penetrate new markets.

By being based in the Kansas City area, Growth was able to obtain contracts with two of the major employers in town, Hallmark Cards and
TWA. Hallmark taught Dunmire a valuable lesson of what markets not
to pursue.

For Hallmark, Growth machined a delicate, high-precision part for
a quality pen and pencil set. In the aerospace business, Growth had
become accustomed to high profit margins associated with highly specialized contract work. Hallmark was making a proprietary product for
mass production. Growth was thrust into a high-volume competitive
situation in which the original equipment manufacturer could control
price and profitability. By offering high volume, the Growth resources
were tapped to a point at which the company would be forced to accept
a price squeeze or, in effect, go out of business.

TWA, on the other hand, represented the type of market that was ideal.
Before describing Growth Industries's entry into the aircraft aftermarket, let me tell you something about the business of supplying parts for
commercial aircraft. As everyone knows, the design and manufacture
of an aircraft is an enormously expensive undertaking. Only the largest corporations like Boeing or Lockheed Martin undertake manufacturing of new commercial or military aircraft. What everyone doesn't
know is that not all manufacturers of aircraft make money on the sale
of the aircraft they manufacture. "What?" you say. "Why would anyone undertake such an expensive task if they could not make a profit?"
The answer simply lies in the magic word—parts. They make money
selling parts.

An aircraft that might sell for $100 million as a new aircraft might sell
for $1 billion sold part by part. Once an aircraft has been manufac-
tured, its life can almost be endless—provided systematic maintenance

can be performed and the parts are replaced on a routinely scheduled basis. The DC-3 flew continuously for over 50 years as a commercial aircraft.

I'm sure you are wondering why more people don't get into the aircraft parts business. It is not that easy. First, a tremendous investment in high-precision equipment and tooling is required. Second, and more critically, the parts must be certified by the Federal Aviation Administration (FAA) as being equivalent to the original equipment. This is a costly, time-consuming, laborious undertaking. And third, there is potential danger of considerable exposure. If an accident were to occur, the manufacturer of any part in the operating or life support systems of an aircraft could be liable for damages that would bankrupt any but the most substantial and insurance-worthy companies. Growth Industries circumvents problem three by limiting its production to nonessential parts.

TWA was an outstanding customer. This was in the days of regulated airfares, and TWA was busy making money for a poorly managed, disorganized airline. Their buyers were under tremendous pressure to purchase parts. They had heavy responsibilities with little direct control over their actions by the company. Strategically, Growth Industries was a lavish entertainer, and found a cadre of buyers receptive to their strategy.

There are three letters of the alphabet that cause airlines to push the panic button. Those three letters are AOG, and they stand for aircraft on the ground. When an aircraft is on the ground and not operational, the cost to the airline is astronomical. If an aircraft is AOG due to needing a special part, the airline could afford to pay almost anything for that part, and it would still be only a drop in the bucket compared to lost revenue when the plane is not flying.

How did Growth Industries become an indispensable supplier to TWA? TWA had a lot of AOG aircraft, and Dunmire pushed his people to make heroes out of the purchasing agents. Growth Industries had one of the most talented groups of machinists assembled anywhere. Each was an artist in his own right with the capability to design and make any part imaginable, either from drawings or from cloning the actual part.

Dunmire invested in expensive tooling to make specialized parts. For example, the company might spend $10,000 for tooling to make a special bolt. They might have an order for fifty bolts that they might sell for $60 per bolt, collecting $3,000 for bolts that cost $10,000 to make. Now, let's say they get another order for fifty bolts at $60 per bolt. Since they now have the tooling, they probably can make the bolt for $5. After a few months they will have sold enough bolts to pay for the tooling. At that point, they would be making a phenomenal profit. Not only will the tooling prove to be an outstanding investment but prospective competitors who can't afford to pay $10,000 to sell a handful of bolts are blocked out.

When I started working with Growth Industries, I thought it was ironic that I also had consulted with TWA several years earlier. As I describe in a different chapter, TWA was a poorly managed and inefficient airline in which employees lacked direction and management lacked control. It was an ideal situation for the Growth Industries sales staff, in which the company could ultimately sell to all airlines from the momentum gained through TWA.

Selling to other better-organized airlines was neither easier nor as profitable. Delta, at that time, was a difficult challenge. In contrast to TWA, Delta was a well-organized airline with a tightly managed purchasing department. Their purchasing agents were brutal. They put everything out for bid and then worked their suppliers against one another by seeing if they could get the losing bidder to rebid below the price of the winning bidder. Going after Delta's business was not the way for Growth to be successful.

Sales played an extremely important role in Dunmire's success at Growth Industries. Dunmire's mentoring in prison was reading Dale Carnegie's book *How to Make Friends and Influence People*. Dunmire was sent to prison with a fifty-year sentence. After two years—with the warden, the prison chaplain, and two members of the parole board strongly in his corner—Dunmire was paroled. Dunmire knew how to sell!

Dunmire was a voracious reader. His tastes ran from six or seven daily newspapers to technical books on business and economics, to dozens of trade publications, to advertising flyers, to pop psychology books, and to omnipresent how-to articles found in the backs of seat pouches on airplanes. He was also a sponge who constantly absorbed information and ideas from others, whether they were professionals, artisans, taxi drivers, or people he met casually. He required his employees to fly first class because of what they might learn from business passengers and airline employees who make up the largest percentage of patrons in first class.

Dunmire was also a loquacious raconteur, who at the slightest whim could take off on a treatise of innumerable different topics. With his assortment of information, he sprinkled his topics with facts, near facts, perceptions, and intuitions, leading to firm conclusions. One of his favorite topics was sales and sales strategies.

Sales Strategies

In looking to hire or develop people with sales personalities who can be great performers, Dunmire searched for ambitious people with competitive drive who intuitively were masters of manipulation. He sorted the manipulative salespeople into two groups: those you can control and those you cannot control. He found candidates through ads or just people he met on the street or in bars. Before he hired someone, he would spend unlimited time in different settings getting to know the person and letting the person know him. He would never hire a person he couldn't control, but he admitted that a good con person could sometimes con him into hiring him or her.

Dunmire explained his sales philosophy to me:

> Growth Industries has always tried to hire and/or develop people with sales personalities who can be great performers. We don't hire sales engineers. We want ambitious people with competitive drive. We want them to use manipulative sales strategies, but they also must be able to establish and maintain close relationships with their customers, much as IBM did with their data center managers. We recognize going in that sales personalities are not always easy to handle, but ultimately, they must be controllable. Just like a television performer. They are 'programmed' and they must follow a script. They are like the old IBM salesman. They give the illusion of being very knowledgeable and independent,

but they are following a carefully designed script that has been dictated daily.

The ultimate sales goal was for the Growth salespeople to develop bonding relationships with buyers. In effect, the goal was to create a series of "monopolies" with specific buyers. Dunmire mentioned that Denise, one of his best salespersons, was able to establish a monopoly even with one of her Delta Airline buyers simply by playing up to him, acknowledging that he was being tough and could even beat up on Dunmire, which made everyone at Delta feel good and solidified Growth's position with them.

Specifically, Dunmire described a formula for rewarding positive actions of customers toward Growth Industries:

> We are big on entertainment. We want our customers to understand that their actions on our behalf are recognized and rewarded. We want them to know that we both want and appreciate their business. We are persistent in asking for business. Each sale is followed up by the salesperson sending a note or making a telephone call. We let the customer know how valuable it was for the salesperson or how it allowed the salesperson to do something special for a family member.

Survival

Dunmire tried to build what he referred to as a *basic company*, which can survive any financial crisis. He described basic companies as having the following characteristics:

- Disciplined companies that can rise to challenge and competition

- Entrepreneurial companies with strong, decisive leaders and a lean work force
- Companies that have developed quasi-monopolistic markets that allow high profit margins
- Sales-oriented companies that know how to exploit the gullibility of others
- Objective companies that know how to minimize risk
- People-oriented companies that understand their employees and know how to control and direct them

Dunmire was a firm believer in the economic theory that major depressions and recessions come in cycles, and as poorly managed companies fail, well-managed companies feast on the spoils. One source of his vision is attributed to Peter Drucker's five conditions for survival of an enterprise described in the preface.

In implementing his survival methodology, Dunmire goes on to explain:

> Growth Industries is a very disciplined organization. We work hard at it. We are like a combat organization. We don't have competitors. We have pretenders. We have carved out a niche that precludes competitors. We carved the niche through discipline. Even without competitors, we continue to be disciplined. We don't want to give up our advantage.

In discussing sales, we learned about Dale Carnegie's influence on Dunmire. The other important influence was Niccolò Machiavelli and his reference to assigning blame and instilling fear. Dunmire routinely instilled fear and blame as a reaction to undesirable behavior by any of his staff. In looking at his own behavior, he recognized that one of his early failings was a lack of fear leading to such foolish actions as robbing a bank. He certainly learned the value of fear in prison.

Management

Dunmire's only management training was in the military. Dunmire looked at the practice of instilling fear and blame as an obligation, much like Gregory Peck in the World War II movie *Twelve O'Clock High*. Gregory Peck was assigned to lead a shoddy bombing crew. His crew was almost in rebellion but ultimately learned that his discipline led to their safety.

Dunmire instilled fear and blame whenever an obvious infraction or misjudgment occurred from one of his employees. The punishment was direct and intended to have an impact without being harsh or unusual. With the caveat that punishment should be dealt with at its occurrence, it sometimes took place publicly, something that clearly is not recommended by most management pundits. Dunmire considered alternatives, but he decided that his decision was the best alternative.

Discipline was paramount at Growth Industries. As Dunmire explained,

> To initiate discipline, you go through something like boot camp. No one can live forever in boot camp, so you have a system of procedures and group cohesion processes to sustain the discipline. When the discipline breaks down, you almost go back to boot camp. I use the analogy of the guy spinning plates. Just when the discipline plate starts to slow down, I put on my "mean" Del Dunmire hat and give the sticks a few more turns.

There was never any question about who ran Growth Industries. In taking time to hire people, Dunmire made clear that candidates understood his management style and actions. He also differentiated where to anticipate discipline issues:

> In any organization of any size, you have two groups of workers. Your direct labor group and your support group. They are often referred to as direct and indirect labor. I like to call then productive and non-productive.
>
> The secret to success in manufacturing is to make sure that your non-productive people don't make your productive people unproductive. A direct-labor job is fairly task oriented and repetitive. The job keeps a worker motivated. Plus, you can easily measure direct labor efficiency and productivity. Support people are behind the line performing a variety of non-measurable tasks.

Even when I was consulting with Growth Industries, I knew Dunmire's management style was out of step with the rest of the world. Although I interviewed all candidates, Dunmire had his own system of spending time getting to know a candidate and letting the candidate know Dunmire. Even with the care Dunmire took in evaluating and indoctrinating candidates, there was high turnover.

Once a new employee truly accepted the Growth way of doing things, the employee invariably became dedicated, loyal, and stable. I came to recognize a pattern in Dunmire hiring extremely intelligent people without college degrees who had worked in hourly-type roles in which someone else had responsibility for directing them.

Dunmire was also extremely loyal, and he rewarded the loyalty of long-term employees with exceptional perks such as expensive automobiles, paid-for vacations, and tickets to sporting and musical events. Employees hosted lavish entertainment events with customers and dignitaries, resulting in bonding friendships with significant community leaders.

Planning

Planning played a critical role in Growth Industries. Whether training employees for their sales roles, planning a party, or determining management strategies and projects, Dunmire was an inveterate planner.

> Successful businesses plan continuously to anticipate the day-to-day contingencies that are likely to impact the businesses. For that reason, I have structured Growth Industries so that I will deal directly with midlevel managers and bypass senior managers. In my chain of command, senior managers serve in staff roles as advisors, general planners, and strategists—feeding information to me.
>
> I don't allow my managers to do much long-range planning. We operate as if we are in a survival mode, with little tolerance for mistakes. We have formal meetings in which midlevel managers have specific skills and job expectations and my job is to make myself available and to monitor the system.

When I first discovered Dunmire's approach to bypassing senior management, I was shocked. I always envisaged senior managers holding midlevel managers accountable. Then I realized that he wasn't really bypassing senior managers. The senior managers were in the same meeting and could intervene and contribute to the planning. When the meeting was over, everyone was on the same page.

What I discovered later was equally shocking. In his first position as a line manager, Harold Geneen, as executive vice president of Raytheon, was able to eliminate a communication bottleneck by inviting division managers, who were accountable for performance, to the monthly meetings of group vice presidents. From these meetings, everyone was on the same page. Del Dunmire and Harold Geneen, both outstanding managers, I discovered, were on the same page.

Dunmire was always looking to create monopolistic advantages. The Bowmar oven, a major acquisition that Dunmire engineered through careful planning and negotiation, boosted sales dramatically. The Bowmar oven in the Lockheed L-1011 aircraft only fit into L-1011s. Lockheed manufactured several thousand L-1011s over a ten-year period up to 1980, and the Bowmar Company made a fortune as the original equipment manufacturer. They were set up to maintain their equipment but not to address the replacement parts market.

The replacement business necessitated additional costs of warehousing, special manufacturing, and hiring personnel to maintain what would amount to a very small segment of their business. Once Lockheed stopped production of the L-1011, the profitability for Bowmar essentially ceased. Through intense planning and preparation, the Bowmar addition allowed Growth Industries to create a monopoly that made millions of dollars for years beyond their acquiring costs.

Dunmire realized a need to have expertise in various areas of business and investing. Much of his education was gained from dialogue with his consultants, which included me and three outside CPAs, a personal lawyer, and a corporate lawyer. As such, my role with Growth Industries was unique. I interviewed his key people and had a good grasp of the various parts of the organization. We obviously spent much time discussing company issues, but time was spent also talking about the fields of psychology, business, management, and politics. As Dunmire explained:

> I avidly learn from the people around me, whether they are top professionals or taxicab drivers. In one way or another, I pay for the services, by either paying consulting fees, giving business to those who share information with me, or by a generous approach to tipping.

Dunmire loved to talk and be the center of a group. He had interesting and humorous stories to tell, often ending in an object lesson. It was obvious that he enjoyed others knowing that Growth Industries had its own psychologist, and Dunmire often deferred to me during a discourse. One of his favorite movies was the first *Airplane* in which two hippies are talking "jive talk," and Barbara Billingsley is interpreting what they said. When Dunmire would be describing something to a group and seeing blank faces, he would often say, "Jim A. is my interpreter. Tell them what I mean, Jim."

As much as he enjoyed talking, Del was also an excellent strategic listener. Meetings with strangers, particularly with those in authority or those he met on flights while he sat in first class, were treated as great sources of potential information. He was empathic and a good judge of a person's mood. He developed his own theories and names to explain behavior. For example, he had a homeostasis "balance" theory that recognized when a person seemed unusually cheerful or depressed.

He felt a father-figure responsibility to his employees and even to his psychologist.

I had carte blanche to do anything I wanted, and most of my time was spent developing relationships with Dunmire and his key people. I introduced group dynamics and D-Group (leaderless T-Group) concepts, which Dunmire quickly accepted and initiated. I sat in on various group meetings, which I found to be participative, focused, and relevant. Once Dunmire understood and accepted my mission, he made sure to remove any hurdles to its implementation.

For a person who came from humble beginnings, Dunmire was an extravagant spender and tipper. It obviously did not come easily, but it was a strategic move to create an image as a big spender. He felt it gave him a tremendous edge over others afraid to spend. He felt that every dollar he spent had a purpose that would pay great dividends without knowing exactly when or how.

Dunmire gave a wonderful example of the purpose behind his spending:

> My manufacturing company is really a marketing company. We can make the finest precision parts in the world, but if we can't sell them at a worthwhile profit, we might as well close the doors. As a marketing company, we have always spent a great deal of money on entertainment. A lot of companies spend money on entertainment, but we absolutely provide our guests with an ultimate experience. For one thing, the servers and people responsible for providing the entertainment are tipped up front as well as at the conclusion of the entertainment anywhere from two to ten

times more than they would normally expect. As you can imagine, waiters and waitresses will almost get into fights to serve me, or one of my salespeople, as a customer. We want the entertainment experience—whether it's dining, an outing, or an event—to be a memorable experience that our guests would never permit themselves to indulge because of the cost. It is something they are likely to remember for a long time.

Dunmire was an unusually thorough planner, whether planning the acquisition of the Bowmar oven or planning a casual dinner party. Dunmire had a favorite expression: "the 2 percent solution," which was based on the name of a Sherlock Holmes movie. His planning strategy was to gather himself and relevant employees to make a 100 percent commitment to the plan at hand. Once the plan was finalized, Dunmire personally added his additional 2 percent to make sure the plan was more than perfect.

Although Dunmire made a fortune in business, he also was a successful land investor. Prior to developing his master plan, he contacted George Lehr, the banker who called his loan in 1979, forcing him to put Growth Industries into bankruptcy. Dunmire was interested in following the model of the J. C. Nichols Company in Kansas City, the developers of the Plaza shopping center, the first major shopping center in America. George Lehr evaluated investments exactly as J. C. Nichols evaluated them in a previous generation, buying land far out from the city and waiting for the city to move out to the land.

Dunmire started investing with his standard investment philosophy: buy low when properties are cheap. Dunmire bought approximately four mostly contiguous square miles of farmland, on both sides of the state line separating Kansas and Missouri. He also bought around fifty properties in the rural town of Harrisonville, Missouri. Some of his acreage held gas wells that provided service to adjacent communities. He ultimately sold his wells for a $10 million profit and sold many of his farms for significant gains. He saw the Harrisonville project as a long-range endeavor to keep him active and a legacy for his heirs.

Dunmire saw successful business as simply dealing with basics. He felt the country would eventually revolt from the technology generation and look to identify with basic living in the past. He saw Harrisonville as a sort of Knotts Berry Farm that would take patrons to a past generation.

As Dunmire disengaged from Growth Industries and his son Mark took over the active management of the business, I stopped working with the company. Dunmire and I remained friends, and we saw each other regularly, usually discussing one of his ideas or a current crisis. He was divorced for a second time and actively dating.

Del Dunmire died of pneumonia July 5, 2016, at the age of eighty-two. His obituaries in the *Kansas City Star* and *Wall Street Journal* were both thorough and enlightening about his career. Following his instructions, his family bought him a plain pine casket and hauled it in the back of a GMC pickup truck to his farm in Drexel, Missouri. They buried him next to his son, James Michael, who died in a 1987 car accident.

Dunmire was an uncanny predictor of economic trends. He was an avid reader and adept at plying knowledge from his consultants and associates. As an investor, he always bought low and sold high. Dunmire attributed his financial success to simply following basic guidelines. In times of financial crisis, his mantra was always "a return to the basics."

Around the turn of the century, with technology changing the face of the economy, Dunmire foresaw a serious recession on the horizon. He also saw a great opportunity for knowledgeable entrepreneurs.

Garry N. Drummond, The Drummond Company

Heman Drummond began a small drift mining operation on family land near Jasper, Alabama, in 1935, eventually expanding into strip mining with the assistance of his three older sons—Donald, Segal, and Garry. Coal was mined and delivered by the sons. Transactions were handled through a cigar box.

Heman Drummond died in 1956, leaving the company to all five of his sons, including Larry and John, and two daughters, with oversight by his wife. Garry Drummond joined the company full-time in 1961 following his graduation in civil engineering from the University of Alabama. Larry Drummond joined later in the 1960s after graduating with accounting and law degrees from the University of Alabama.

I first learned about Drummond from headlines in the *Birmingham News* when they were being sued by the federal government for allegations of excessive spending on business travel and expenses. The allegations were not confirmed, and the whole issue eventually died.

I became acquainted with Drummond through my association as a consultant to Arthur Young & Company (AY) in Birmingham, Alabama, that served as a consultant to Drummond. By the time I became involved with Drummond, they were the largest private coal company in America and one of the largest companies in Alabama. The growth was attributed to the sales efforts of Garry Drummond in signing a contract to deliver $100 million in coal each year for ten years to Ataka & Co. in Tokyo, Japan, and winning a fifteen-year contract to deliver two million tons of coal per year at a top price to the Alabama Power Company's coal-fired electrical generation plants.

The Drummond Company's growth was accomplished with Garry Drummond as president and Larry Drummond as head of administration. The other three brothers had minor positions. Garry Drummond was outgoing, confident, and inquisitive. Often impulsive and impatient, he was always looking to understand and improve situations. He was active in social, volunteer, philanthropic, and political activities, and the company was recognized for its heavy emphasis on entertaining customers, politicians, and employees. The Drummond Company owned a hunting lodge in Georgia and country club golf courses in Alabama, Florida, and California—all available for entertainment. Each year the company invited business and political friends to a gala hunting weekend at a lodge in Mexico with an unlimited supply of quail.

In writing about Del Dunmire, the owner of Growth Industries, I described how he orchestrated entertainment events to be "unforgettable experiences" for his guests. By my living in La Quinta, California, Garry Drummond invited me to attend several parties he held at Rancho La Quinta Country Club. I can attest that these excursions were "unforgettable experiences" for his guests.

Garry understood the value of business and political relationships in establishing monopolies early in his entrepreneurial career. A friend and early mentor, James (Jim) Walter, was a legendary entrepreneur in the Southeast and the founder of Jim Walter Homes in Florida and Jim Walter Industries in Alabama, a leading producer of metallurgical coal for the global steel industry. After adding an assortment of building materials companies related to his home construction business, Jim

Walter sold his assets to Kohlberg, Kravis, Roberts (KKR) for $3.3 billion dollars in 1988.

Garry Drummond never thought small. He formed close relationships with Alabama Power executives. His sale of two million tons of coal per year for fifteen years gave Drummond a guaranteed monopolistic income of over $2 billion. Garry Drummond made sure that Drummond was never short of working capital!

With its rapid growth, Drummond looked to Arthur Young both for consultation and as a resource for filling top administration roles. In 1981, Joe Nicholls, the AY partner in charge of tax accounting, was hired as the Drummond senior vice president in charge of finance, a staff position, and he brought Pat Willingham with him to serve as the head of financial operations. As I describe in a later chapter on Arthur Young, Willingham brought me into Drummond to assist him in developing his staff, introducing me into a consulting role with Drummond that continued for almost thirty years.

Once I started working with Willingham, Bert Pribbenow, the sales vice president, contacted me to work with his sales group. Pribbenow was a brilliant person in his early thirties who was from Jasper and a graduate of Vanderbilt University. Pribbenow joined Drummond out of college as Garry Drummond's assistant; his job included picking up Garry Drummond's laundry and running personal favors but also establishing relationships with Garry Drummond's business and personal contacts.

Jasper was the home of William Bankhead, speaker of the House of Representatives during the Franklin Roosevelt presidency, and actress Tallulah Bankhead's father. Jasper was home to a strong political tradition that helped establish the Drummond Company's influence in state and national politics.

Pribbenow was a knowledgeable, creative salesman, but he was a laissez-faire manager. George Wilbanks, Bert's top salesman, served the same role for Pribbenow as Pribbenow served for Garry Drummond. Pribbenow was responsible for a sales office at the Mobile port that was disorganized and inefficient, and he was responsible for a quality control function with thirty lab techs reporting to one reluctant supervisor. The department was staffed with excellent people, and Pribbenow was happy to have me help him structure a workable organization.

Surface Mining

When I joined Drummond, they had thirty surface mines churning out coal on a 24/7 basis, supporting sales throughout the United States, Japan, and Europe. Through a system of barges, coal flowed from tributaries to the Black Warrior River to an exclusive dock at the Mobile port for international shipments.

An Alabama surface coal mine in which coal is mined through a dragline is an awesome sight. Alabama is at the foot of the Appalachian Mountains, with narrow seams of coal close to the surface running for miles. In the initial mine design, every step is determined, including the ultimate reclamation of the mine, which could become a farm, a lake, a mountain, or any combination. Unlike horror stories that abound, a surface mine allocates a percentage of coal sales to guarantee the successful reclamation of the mine.

A surface mine consists of a dragline up to six stories high with a shovel attachment that with each scoop moves dirt equivalent in space to a three-room house. With each swing, the dragline "walks" as the "feet" of the dragline are alternately thrust forward. When a large part of the dirt over the seam is removed, dynamite is distributed and exploded throughout the exposed seam, to be scooped up with peripheral equipment into rows of waiting trucks. When a dragline moves to a new mine, it walks to the new mine with its staff retinue taking down and replacing power lines blocking the path.

In 1981, my daughter, Libby, enrolled at the University of Arizona in Tucson. After dropping her off at the dorm, my wife, Rena, and I decided to look over the town. We ran into a couple who also brought their daughter to the college. In talking with the father, he told me that Tucson had a gigantic copper mine and that at the copper mine was the largest shovel imaginable used to scoop up the copper. We visited the mine, and we were impressed with the shovel. Years later, when visiting one of the Drummond mines, I learned that the very shovel I saw in Tucson was being used as peripheral equipment with the Drummond dragline.

After settling into my work with Pat Willingham and Bert Pribbenow, I learned that both Garry and Larry Drummond were eager to have their assessments. Once those assessments and feedbacks were completed, I routinely had individual discussions with Garry or Larry Drummond concerning my activities. In a confidential management review that I prepared on August 1, 1982, for the Drummond brothers, one section dealt specifically with the relationship between Garry and Larry Drummond:

> The relationship with Garry and Larry in the past has been complementary, but it is now becoming competitive . . . Any successful compromise or reorganization must assure both Garry and Larry that each of them will have some con-

trol over the actions of the other that he finds undesirable. Garry feels that Larry can be manipulated by his staff and that he is not assertive enough in directing them. Larry feels that Garry is too dominant in making decisions, too quick to act without the facts and too harsh in his judgment of others.

The brothers were both essential to the organization, and their relationships did remain complementary. Larry Drummond was involved in addressing administrative and operations issues and in supporting my involvement in operations.

One person I had not interviewed was Donald (Don) Baxter, the vice president of operations, with the bulk of employees under his control. Larry Drummond knew that Baxter did not want to see me and had always arranged to be busy. Baxter, who was in his late thirties, had worked his way up into management with the Peabody Coal Company, America's largest coal company. He had been in his position with Drummond through its period of growth. Larry said he wanted me to not let Baxter off the hook and to wait him out.

My visit with Baxter was surprising. Baxter turned out to be some type of genius with immediate recall who single-handedly coordinated the planning and overall management of all Drummond mines. He had thirty mine managers reporting to him directly. He had daily briefings with the engineers carrying out plans and the mine managers running the mines. Each morning, he rode in a helicopter to visually check each mine to gain a clear picture of progress.

I came to recognize that Baxter was a one-man band and that the company would be in serious trouble without him. He had promoted two people into key supervisory roles, but even they mostly carried out things he directed. Not only did he control the operations, but he met daily with the transportation coordinators in sales. Without his intervention, transportation would have serious difficulties.

Baxter and I bonded quickly. I helped him to gain greater perspective and strategies for working with some of his people. We were also able to develop some group training sessions that were well received. Baxter was like a sponge. He educated me about his job, and then he picked my brain to broaden his perspective.

My relationship with Baxter was also an education. I realized that the growth of the company was due to Garry Drummond's aggressive management in negotiating the sales and in pushing the growth of the company. I knew that multiple professional staff had come from Arthur Young, but Pat Willingham was the only "true" manager. I further realized that the company's infrastructure was inadequate for its size and that Don Baxter was plugging the dike as a formal structure evolved.

Underground Mining

In 1982, Drummond acquired the Alabama By-Products Company (ABC) in Birmingham, Alabama, from its elderly local stockholders. The company consisted of five underground mines and a coke plant that processed coal into foundry coke used in steel casting operations. Overnight, Drummond was confronted with running a complex operation in which it lacked experience and expertise. Charles Adair retired in 1982 as president of the Mead Corporation's Iron and Metals Group to become vice president and assistant to Garry Drummond. With the

ABC acquisition, Adair became president and CEO of ABC, a position he held until his retirement in 1989.

The hiring of Charles Adair was a fortuitous decision. He was a highly competent person with executive experience in managing large mining-related enterprises. He struck out immediately to evaluate all aspects of ABC's operations and ways to integrate overlapping functions with Drummond. We had already established a compatible relationship, and my first major project was to evaluate ABC management and identify potential problem areas.

My working relationship with Charles Adair was one of the most satisfying in my career. Very quickly, multiple management and infrastructure problems emerged. Many couldn't be resolved because of Drummond's inadequate infrastructure. Under guidance from Adair, I undertook dozens of significant action research projects (in addition to the assessment program) that led to an understanding of problems and issues that could be addressed systematically. Over a two-year period, Charles Adair was able to restructure and standardize most corporate systems.

ABC was owned by a small group of local owners, none of whom had an active role in the business. Howard Withers was the longtime president of the coke operation, which was centralized by Withers's control over all functions. The company had a sterling reputation for product quality, but high overhead and a conservative approach to sales limited profits. Withers's retirement, combined with standardizing operations and administration and the promotion of a sales-oriented president, led to ABC becoming the leading coke processor it is today.

The coal mines by contrast were highly decentralized, with total control vested with the individual mine managers. Ed Sherriff, the president, was new to ABC, but he had a long career in mining management. He was showing systematic progress in improving systems and procedures. Sherriff had never been underground at any of the mines, and he depended on his operations manager for liaison with the mine managers.

I was responsible for systematically assessing the management people in the mines. In an interview with a supervisor in maintenance, I was told that a thievery ring, operating under a key executive, sold equipment on order from other mines in the region. I explained to the person I was interviewing that our session was confidential and that I couldn't tell Drummond management, but he agreed to inform Charles Adair. The principals were fired, ostensibly without cause.

Don Baxter had already assumed the role of vice president for ABC operations, and he quickly mastered a critical overview of underground mining. Most of the mine managers were mining engineers with substantial experience. Bonuses were based on performance, and the mines were profitable.

Safety engineers theoretically could close a mine, but mine managers could override safety decisions. One of the safety engineers told me that his primary mission was keeping the soda machine full. Don Baxter systematically addressed issues of mismanagement in the mines that might have existed for generations. A mine fatality, caused by a safety violation, could have been devastating to the company.

Aside from my role in assessing individual management personnel, I was instrumental in undertaking two major action research and implementation projects involving the Drummond management information services (MIS) function and the accounting function. Major problems in each functional area had to be resolved before integrating with comparable ABC functions, which also had their own major problems. As production in the ABC mines diminished, I was responsible for establishing a viable reduction-in-force system for terminating section foremen.

Recognizing that both underground and surface mines were aging, and that production was diminishing, Garry Drummond approved studies that resulted in two gigantic strategic projects. The first was the development of the Shoal Creek underground mine in 1994, which was the largest underground mine in America at that time and which is still actively operated today.

The second was a long-term project headed by Bert Pribbenow leading to the opening of the La Loma mine in Colombia, South America that has been producing about twenty-five million tons of coal annually since 1994. Through Pribbenow's initial efforts, an arrangement was made whereby the Colombian government in partnership allowed Drummond to build the mine on forty square miles of land with quarters nearby sheltering 1,000 Colombian soldiers available to protect the mine. Drummond also built a 100-mile railroad track to transport the coal to a shipping area in Santa Marta on the Colombian northern coast.

Although I was involved with both long-term projects, I endured a five-year hiatus from my consulting role with Drummond starting in mid-1990 to mid-1995. Following Charles Adair's decision to retire, Garry Drummond hired a top executive from Consol Energy to join Drummond as president and to report to Garry Drummond as CEO. He was given a five-year contract. Shortly after his hiring, I was in-

formed that my services were no longer needed. Almost five years to
the day I was terminated, I was informed that the president's contract
was not renewed and asked if I would return. When I returned, I was
immediately thrust into revisiting the mines and consulting in Colombia.

From the start, Don Baxter had taken the lead on both the Shoal Creek
and the Colombia projects. Unlike Shoal Creek, the ABC mines were
continuous flow mines where coal was extracted through pillared, often
narrow, shafts with low ceilings referred to as low coal. Shoal Creek was
designed to diversify production utilizing the longwall methodology,
a new automation technology incorporating line slicing, rather than a
drilling. Longwall was safer and faster, yielding a higher percentage of
coal recovery.

Baxter's goal for ABC mines was to create knowledgeable, self-sufficient managers who followed standardized, measurable procedures using trained, competent supervisors and union workers. By the time
I left the company, significant progress had been made toward those
goals and operations proceeded in a routine manner.

Long-wall was another story. All long-wall managers had to be recruited, mainly from larger companies in upper Appalachia. I interviewed
all candidates, and individuals with skills beyond the Drummond staff
were hired. Hiring outsiders from the north is one thing; integrating
them is something else. A major group dynamics effort facilitated the
integration.

Colombian Mining

The Colombian operation was—and is—an impressive enterprise. Coal
seams of most Alabama mines are thin, measured in inches to a foot or

so. They are either surface or underground mines and require a complicated process of recovering coal mixed with rock that goes through a washing procedure. The Colombian coal seams are up to ten or more feet thick and are mined by shovels punching into seams and scooping clean coal into gigantic truck beds that are unloaded onto railroad coal cars that travel directly to the Santa Marta Port.

I spent three distinct periods consulting in Colombia. The first period was in 1995–1997, shortly after the La Loma mine was first opened, with Drummond people flown in on a large private jet from Birmingham; the second in 1999–2000, when the mine was consolidating activities in Colombia; and the third in 2005–2006, when Colombians were dominating the workforce.

Initially, my efforts involved assisting in the selection of operations, engineering, and administrative personnel, mostly from Drummond, to assume permanent positions in Colombia. I also assisted in assessing a former CIA agent to create and oversee a security division and in the hiring of a former general in the Colombian military. My subsequent efforts were focused on assisting in filling positions with native Colombians and in assisting in the hiring of expatriates with international mining experience.

With the Revolutionary Armed Forces of Colombia (FARC) rebels active throughout Drummond's management of the mine, security was always a high priority. During a period of massive kidnappings and murders, many Colombians chose to spend their days off at the mine rather than risk travel to their homes. The coal trains were attacked regularly, and a trainman was killed in one of the attacks.

In traveling to Colombia, the established procedure was to fly in a scheduled large private jet from Birmingham to Santa Marta, where the Drummond shipping port was located approximately two miles from the airport along a road bordered heavily with vegetation. To continue to the mine approximately 100 miles south of the airport, a large propeller plane flew directly to a landing area at the mine. To travel from the airport to the port, one of three random routes were taken to avoid FARC confrontation: motorboat, helicopter, or armored car led by a soldier on a motorcycle and followed by a Jeep filled with armed soldiers.

Although Bert Pribbenow was the genius behind the Colombia mine, he never had a chance to realize the great success of his brainchild. He developed an inoperable brain tumor and died in his mid-thirties. Pribbenow was among the most optimistic, considerate people I have ever known. He was taking steroid medication and did not show any outward evidence of his illness. A week prior to his death, he took George Wilbanks and me to lunch, never once complaining and even jocularly offering his condolence for some of the company issues that he knew we would be facing.

The Drummond brothers were all golfers. When the bottom fell out of the price of phosphate, Garry Drummond decided to transform a Lakeland, Florida, phosphate mine into a country club. Some of the group that created the golf course claimed jokingly that it "glowed in the dark." Multiple successful country clubs followed including Rancho La Quinta and Andalusia in the Palm Springs area and Old Overton in Birmingham.

Don Baxter retired from Drummond in 2006, but he maintained an ad hoc consulting relationship. Garry Drummond often sought his advice. My involvement with the company also diminished, but I also was involved in ad hoc assignments for Garry Drummond.

Garry Drummond was active in state and national professional organizations, and he was a founder of the American Coal Foundation. He was a longtime member of the University of Alabama Board of Trustees. He won awards as outstanding alumnus, and he was inducted into numerous honorary societies.

In 2014, Drummond sold 10 percent of the company to Japanese investors for $1 billion. In 2016, Garry Drummond was written up in *Forbes* as the richest man in the state of Alabama. He died unexpectedly on July 13, 2016, at the age of seventy-eight. He was preceded in death by his brothers Don, Segel, and Larry, and his two sisters.

The success of the Drummond Company is related directly to Garry Drummond's forceful leadership and his social, business, and political connections in representing the company. His major sales accomplishment in Japan was related directly to Drummond being able to demonstrate their honesty and reliability to deliver what they promised. Garry Drummond thought and planned big, and he was willing to take the financial risks that projected the company to its $10 billion value in 2014.

Garry Drummond's commitment to the Drummond Company was 100 percent, meaning that he often spread himself thinly and initiated actions he could not resolve. He had Larry Drummond to cover administration, and both brothers afforded latitude to people like Don Baxter and Charles Adair with long-term perspectives and organizational skills.

As it was a private company with multiple family members as stock-holders, an important decision was made that precluded offspring from active participation in the company. With Garry Drummond's dom-inating leadership style and sales coups, the company used lucrative salary, benefits, and bonus considerations to employ top professional employees and to build excellent union relationships. Drummond was a company that emerged from a cigar-box mentality into one of the largest and most successful private companies in America.

David J. Noble, American Equity Investment Life Insurance Company

On May 31, 2017, I was at the Iowa Events Center in Des Moines, Iowa, for a celebration of the life of David J. (Dave) Noble, who died on April 16, 2017, at the age of eighty-five. Noble and various compa-nies with which he was involved were an integral part of my consulting career for almost fifty years.

General United Life Insurance Company

In the summer of 1961, General United Life was formed in West Des Moines, Iowa, with the consolidation of five small life insurance com-panies into General United. General United was owned by a holding company in Chicago. The CEO and a major stockholder of General United was Jack Schroeder, a former candidate for governor and the president/owner of one of the companies being merged. The chief op-erating officer was Dave Noble, who had also been the COO of one of the merged companies.

Noble and Schroeder had the frantic task of sorting through employees from five companies with the same titles to pick one final staff. On a routine call from a reinsurance agent from the Business Men's Assurance Company (BMA) in Kansas City, a client of mine, Schroeder and Noble pleaded with him to help them select the best people. When he told them that BMA had a psychologist who does that sort of thing, they clambered to get my telephone number.

I arrived in Des Moines with apprehension. I was not a hatchet man, but I felt that the employees wouldn't understand my role. Much to my surprise, I discovered that all the employees were looking forward to my arrival. Prior to my coming, it was a bloodbath with everyone in conflict with everyone else. At least I would be an objective, outside professional.

Schroeder was a smiling, outgoing person in his late thirties who had a meteoric rise through the state legislature to his nomination to run for governor. Throughout his life when he was asked "How are you?" he always answered with "Happy." He, as president, along with his sales manager-to-be, spent a year selling stock in the insurance company they were to run.

Dave Noble was twenty-nine years old; five feet, seven inches tall; intense; and alert to what was going on around him. He was a college dropout who got started early in the insurance business and who quickly mastered the details of how to run an insurance company. He laid out a plan with a successful insurance salesman to buy a small company that Noble would run for him. By the time I met Noble, Jack Schroeder had already agreed to have Noble as his right-hand man.

I quickly did assessments on Schroeder and Noble, and then I started to interview the various candidates. I came to Des Moines every two weeks at the beginning and then came once a month for three or four days. Schroeder was an early morning person who greeted me for breakfast every morning at 6:30. Dave Noble was a night owl who liked to close bars, and I was usually in bed by midnight. I worried about my health and finally set some limits to my availability.

Schroeder and I mostly talked about general issues. Noble pinned me down for the specifics of any issue. From the start, there was mutual respect. Noble accepted my expertise, and I never doubted his intuition and the accuracy of his perceptions. In our initial assessment session, Noble told me that his goal was to run his own large life insurance company. In our feedback session, I described him as a big fish in a little pond (i.e., so involved with controlling everything that he forfeits perspective). He asked me to help him change.

With the activity generated by Noble, the organization came together quickly. Although there was a surplus of staff, it was recognized that it was best to reorganize cautiously. One area of concern was information technology (then known as data processing). The person heading the department was indecisive, and the department was not organized. On one of my consulting visits, Noble met me at the airport and told me that he ordered the head of data processing to fire half of his staff. He said that if he fired them by the end of the day, he would let the department head choose the ones to leave; otherwise, Noble would choose them. Noble said he wanted me to interview each of the remaining employees to evaluate their morale.

What I found was a group of happy employees who had been frustrated with a disruptive core of fellow employees and a disorganized manager. My point in telling the story is that it is so typical of what I saw for fifty years in Dave Noble—the ability to define a problem and to take an appropriate action.

Once the organization stabilized with systems in place, the company was profitable and growing by the end of the year. At the time, General United had an opportunity to take possession of an Iowa-domiciled company selling automobile insurance to subprime borrowers in Los Angeles. Noble agreed to assume the title of president for one year to stabilize the company. Noble and his family moved to Los Angeles. I consulted with Noble that year as he systematically provided structure and hired two key people. General United chose not to keep the California company, and it was sold.

Within a few years, the Chicago holding company sold General United to a company in Chicago and moved the operation to Chicago. Everything happened quickly without advance notice. Schroeder was a stockholder and came out well monetarily. Noble was abruptly out of a job with not much to show for his efforts in creating a salable asset in General United.

On my last visit to Des Moines, Noble drove me to the airport. I remember vividly his saying that he didn't know how, but he was going to put a company together and that he would give me a call. I told him how much I genuinely enjoyed working with him and wished him well, but I never thought I would see him again.

American Allied Life Insurance Company/ Vulcan Life Insurance Company

Noble called within a year to let me know that he was starting a new insurance company in Birmingham, Alabama, American Allied, and he wanted me to consult with the company. At the time it was a company of ten or twelve, including Jim Gerlach, who started in Noble's first company and now continues to serve on the American Equity board of directors.

It turned out that Noble not only was resourceful but also had access to financial resources. The main resource was Ed Roth, an agent who owned the company that Noble worked with before joining General United. Shortly after the start of American Allied, a merger was arranged with Vulcan Life in Birmingham, a debit insurance company with national coverage in which agents collect premiums door to door each month. With the merger in 1971, Noble became president of Vulcan, selling off the debit business and building a standard life insurance company with a diversified line of products sold in most states through independent agents and with company agents selling to associated groups such as the National Guard.

The merger of American Allied with Vulcan Life was preceded by the retirement of the former president of Vulcan Life. Noble had achieved his goal of having his own life insurance company to run.

Vulcan was the start of a long association with Dave Noble in Birmingham. I traveled to Birmingham each month, assisting Noble to build his organization. Noble was a top-down manager who absolutely controlled and knew what was going on at any time in his organization. At the time I was working with Dave, I also was a psychological consultant for International Telephone & Telegraph (ITT) under Harold Geneen. Noble was a disciple of the no-surprises top-down philosophies of Harold Geneen, which we often discussed. Geneen expected his executives to notify him about impending surprises. Noble usually anticipated surprises even prior to the knowledge of his executives.

When I described Dave as a "big fish in a small pond," I didn't realize that Dave, not unlike Harold Geneen, simply added more resources for observation as the pond got bigger. Dave built strong relationships with his consultants and advisers, giving them latitude and listening carefully to what they said. He also formed close relationships with midlevel managers to keep track of high-level managers.

In every position Dave held, it was common knowledge that he had a "spy" system that included his personal secretary as a coordinator of the system. The unique thing about Dave's spy system was that it was simply to provide him with information. He rarely made an issue from the information he gathered, and his "spies" always knew they were protected.

Noble genuinely went out of his way to help people and to build a network of friends and associates. The auditors of Vulcan were the Big Eight firm Arthur Young & Co. Noble had a close relationship with the managing partner and many of the individual staff.

Noble recommended me to Arthur Young, and I worked as a consultant to them, primarily in Birmingham but also with assignments in New Orleans and Atlanta. He also helped senior Arthur Young staff looking for new assignments by recommending them personally to people he knew. John Matovina, the CEO and chairman of American Equity, started his career as an auditor with Arthur Young in Birmingham, working on the Vulcan account.

Noble's operational mantra was to keep costs down, particularly wages, in order to invest in income-generating applications. He didn't mind paying onetime bonuses. He felt strongly that wages never came down, and it was his job to not let them get out of hand.

The educational level of midlevel managers at Vulcan was below that of other profitable insurance companies that typically hired college-trained people in lower-level positions with an understanding that they would be the top candidates to rise in the company. The people filling midlevel management positions at Vulcan were the people who were promoted from entry ranks who had proven their industriousness and their loyalty.

The fact that Vulcan was a top-down company was compatible with employees being accountable for manually implementing existing systems and procedures. Recognizing the need for future technology, Vulcan invested in talented IT programmers working closely with outside vendors to provide the software to ensure continued growth.

One of Noble's unequivocal goals was to provide excellent service to insured customers and to salesmen. He demanded that telephones be answered by people, not machines, and that no caller was shuffled off without receiving information requested.

Vulcan paid competitive sales commissions. In addition, much management time was spent creating rewards and incentives for sales accomplishments. In all companies with which Noble was involved, the top producers and their designated companions were rewarded with an annual one-week all-expenses paid trip to an exotic international location. Key employees and their spouses also attended, often forming lifelong bonds.

There was never a question among employees concerning leadership. Noble was a dominating presence. At 5:00 p.m., the bar was open for the management group to have a drink with Noble and to share information. The practice was never formalized, but everyone always attended.

Noble's work commitment was total. Most evenings included dining out with staff members or consultants. Before the age of mobile telephones, Noble always carried a massive portable battery telephone system on his nightly excursions. Noble always had a corporate airplane and corporate pilots ready if needed.

The Statesman Group

In 1978, a merger of Vulcan was negotiated with the Statesman Group in Des Moines, an insurance holding company, in which Ed Roth emerged as the chairman and Dave Noble became executive vice president. The Statesman Group was the brainchild of Allen Whitfield, a founder in the Whitfield and Eddy law firm. Harley Whitfield, Allen Whitfield's son and law firm successor, and Dave Noble were lifelong friends. Harley Whitfield was a primary adviser to Noble throughout Noble's career.

Allen Whitfield was a creative entrepreneur. The Statesman Group was the first employee stock ownership plan (ESOP) created in America. In the new structure, Whitfield was able to establish complicated entities and powers of attorney that were legal at the time. With 1 percent of the stock, the law firm maintained controlling interest in the ESOP, affording tax savings and benefits to the principals and a source of continual income for the law firm.

The primary holdings of the Statesman Group were two auto insurers, State Auto of Iowa and State Auto of Indiana, in Des Moines and Indianapolis, and American Life and Casualty Insurance in Fargo, North Dakota. The companies had capable presidents, all of whom were owners before the Statesman Group was assembled as a vehicle to reduce expenses, federal regulations, and potential liabilities.

Each company functioned autonomously. I established consulting relationships with Orval Allen, the president of the Indianapolis company, and Gordon (Tut) Heller, the president of the Fargo company, in which I assessed each president and their executive staffs. Both were receptive to my involvement, but both were running successful, independent organizations with minimal interest in forming a close liaison with the new Statesman management. Allen was in his mid-fifties, but Heller was in his late sixties and scheduled for mandatory retirement. State Auto of Iowa was the smallest of the three companies, and the president had retired at the time of the merger. Dave Noble served as the acting president.

Orval Allen was an outstanding manager. He joined the company early in his career, working under entrepreneurial leaders who created aggressive sales organizations combined with structured, reliable service. One of the cofounders was a World War II general who was described to me as being not too different from General George S. Patton. Allen, by contrast, was an even-keeled, predictable person who always looked at the big picture, understood the business plan, and gained confidence and respect from his staff. The staff I interviewed were competent and experienced.

The company also had a satellite office in Hershey, Pennsylvania, that I visited to assess three promising junior managers. The office had been managed by the general, and Allen laughingly warned me that the woman running the kitchen made sure the general's rules were followed, including rules about when coffee could be served. In my first assessment in the morning, I inadvertently asked if we could get a cup of coffee. When I saw the look of terror on the face of the young man I was interviewing, I knew I asked the wrong question. After some hemming and hawing, he left to plead with the woman in question. I don't know what he said, but he came back with a smile on his face and a cup of coffee. When I first saw the TV sitcom *The Office*, I thought about my visit to Hershey.

State Auto of Iowa was in the Des Moines Building, the headquarters building of the Statesman Group. I spent more time with the Des Moines staff than I did with the other companies. State Auto was a small company, marginally profitable, selling subprime auto insurance. Most of the employees had been with the company for years. The claims department was two people who had worked together for over ten years—a male claims manager and a female claims agent.

One day after arriving in Des Moines, Dave Noble advised me that I needed to get involved with the claims area. The female claims agent hired a female lawyer and filed a sexual harassment charge against the male supervisor. Noble let me read the charge, the documented evidence, and the transcript of recordings of verbal interactions between the two employees. Apparently, through the years, the two were friends who routinely talked trash to each other, much like servicemen with profanity and jocular but profane references. The female agent decided one day to stop such behavior and let her supervisor know that she would no longer participate in such discussions. The supervisor did not accept her request, and his comments to her were secretly recorded and transcribed in the complaint.

The lawsuit sought to refrain trash talk from the supervisor, to increase the agent's pay slightly, and to have me mediate sessions between the two of them. When trash talk is transcribed, the effect is devastating. It took one short mediation to resolve the case. Just think what she could have gained had she filed a lawsuit in today's times.

The gem that came with the merger was American Life and Tut Heller. Heller was an outgoing, friendly, dominating person who stood out in any group with his quick wit, knowledge, and take-charge style. In addition to his being a domineering force in the company, he was active in community affiliations, in entertaining at his country club, and in establishing contacts and relationships in the insurance industry.

Although American Life was a traditional life insurance company, Heller entrepreneurially created a fixed rate annuity product that became the main source of income and growth in the company. Once the product was created, he lined up national marketing organizations (NMOs) to sell the annuities, and he developed a staff to service applications and accounts. Most of the NMO agreements were worked out in a bar, writing on the back of an envelope and figuring out a mutually satisfying commission for the agent. A competent staff was readily available. Fargo was a city with well-educated employees but with limited employment opportunities.

With the autonomy he held in the Statesman Group, Heller was not influenced by the new corporate leadership. With his impending retirement, he knew he would be replaced by Jon Newsome, a rising star in the Statesman Group. Heller negotiated a plan with Dave Noble, whereby he could establish a private office to service personal accounts in a new American Life office in which he was responsible for designing the layout. Before Newsome moved from Des Moines to Fargo, I was on assignment in Fargo. Heller showed me the newly constructed company layout that included his personal office that was three times the size of any of the other offices.

Newsome as president/director of marketing, Terry Reimer as operations director, and Bill Hang as IT manager all arrived together as a new management team. Heller was assigned a small office and left the company after a few months. Under Newsome's leadership, all three of the new additions made outstanding contributions, and the company showed impressive growth.

With the Statesman Group's growth and profitability, a management decision was made to diversify by buying a mortgage company in Atlanta. In reviewing the proposal, the federal government deemed that Statesman would need to acquire four failing savings and loan (S&L) organizations in both Florida and Iowa that were in receivership. As part of the due diligence, I was assigned the task of visiting eight S&L offices to assess the key managers.

The task was a vivid lesson in how not to run a business. Each of the S&Ls was established from the same cookie cutter. None of the managers I interviewed had strong backgrounds of experience for their positions. A majority used outside consultants to evaluate their situations and to help them develop their strategic business plans.

The plans in all cases were the same. The consultants determined that each S&L was struggling due to its limited access to available homes in its restricted geographic areas. They were advised to find homes to mortgage in high growth areas, thus starting the S&L mortgage meltdown of the early 1980s. Once Statesman acquired the failed companies, the federal government sued Statesman for each of the S&L failures, resulting in a lawsuit against the federal government by Statesman. Statesman won the lawsuit with damages approximately ten years after it was filed.

In the mid-1980s, Ed Roth was interested in retiring. Through the ESOP, Dave Noble and Harley Whitfield raised $8 million to buy out Roth's holdings, with Noble becoming chairman and president of the Statesman Group.

American Life and Casualty Company

In 1994, American Life and Casualty, Statesman Life, and Vulcan Life merged into one life insurance company with all operations moving to Des Moines. Jack Schroeder was named president of the company. Both casualty companies were sold. The success of American Life under Jon Newsome's leadership led to his being hired by Equitable Insurance Company to head its annuity division in Des Moines.

In 1994, the Statesman Group was sold to Conseco, Inc., an insurance holding company in Carmel, Indiana. Within a brief period, Conseco shipped the Statesman financial assets (91 percent in annuities) to Carmel and offered jobs (not accepted) to two or three Statesman employees. They did not have Noble sign a noncompete agreement. Noble almost immediately started gathering financing to establish a new annuity company, American Equity Investment Life Insurance Company, not unlike a mythical phoenix to rise from the ashes of American Life and Casualty Company.

American Equity Investment Life Insurance Company

After the company was established, Noble asked me to serve as a consultant. Unlike my typical role, I defined with Noble a limited role in which I would become involved in defining management issues.

One of the smartest moves Noble made was to promote Kevin Wingert from a senior marketing position to president of American Equity. With American Life, Wingert excelled in building a marketing function to support a growing group of NMOs, but he also was a conceptual person eager to bring about constructive changes to move American Equity to a higher level. Wingert and I formed a close relationship in bringing about change. On May 16, 2001, I wrote the following introduction to a proposal for various change strategies that were presented to Noble, Wingert, and Debbie Richardson, chief administration officer:

> American Equity was created to complement the management style Dave Noble used successfully for almost fifty years. The management style requires a strong, dominant leader and a loyal, committed staff responsible for implementing company plans, systems, and procedures.

> Dave recognizes both the strengths and limitations of his management style. He selected Kevin Wingert as a president who both understands the success created by the present system, but who also has the vision and capability to modify past practices to show future growth. Dave asked me to help create an organization that has the potential to succeed ultimately without him. He knows I will not come up with radical ideas that are not consistent with the capabilities of the staff.

> American Equity has a tremendous advantage over previous DJN-run companies. Aside from its current success and momentum, it is blessed with a talented, well-educated blend of experienced and entry staff. The Company is not broke, and the proposed strategic reorganization and training program is a long-range program that will not disrupt the present direction and momentum of the Company.

The management world has changed dramatically over the past fifteen years. Layers upon layers of management have proven to be redundant and obsolete. With few exceptions, clerks are not employable. We are in a systems/technology world that requires employees to understand and manage technical resources. Ideal organizations are flat in structure with a few managers overseeing the individuals or teams of individuals that implement the systems that drive the daily business.

In a traditional top-down organization, one of the most difficult tasks in seeking change is getting established managers to give up rigid authority or at least to plan for greater management participation from their staffs. Kevin Wingert and Debbie Richardson were instrumental in fostering gradual systematic changes in the organizational structure as Dave disengaged.

Both professional HR and IT managers were hired. Effective services evolved as the company filled key positions with qualified candidates,

Wingert left the company to start his own NMO, and John Matovina eventually assumed the position. As the company grew, new hires met higher standards of educational attainment and technical competence.

My involvement with American Equity was the last of a long, satisfying history with Dave Noble. As I moved toward retirement and Noble disengaged, my contacts with American Equity ended, except for an occasional minor crisis contact. American Equity has continued to grow into one of the country's leading fixed rate annuity insurer, a tribute to Noble's vision and commitment.

Noble's strength was in his total commitment to the enterprise and in his dominant presence. Not unlike Harold Geneen, his spy system guaranteed no surprises. Noble ran pay-as-you-go companies with limited investment capital. At the same time, he spent money wisely on maximizing contributions of outside consultants in financial, accounting, actuarial, and human resources areas. He diverted capital into competitive sales compensation and benefits, and he recognized needs for keeping up with new technology. He rewarded loyalty and built long-lasting personal and professional relationships with employees, sales representatives, and outside consultants.

Three Companies: Comments

My decision to write a memoir evolved from a series of coincidences. The first was having three of my long-term managerial clients die in a relatively short time and subsequently acknowledging consistent similarities in their entrepreneurial style and in their management commitments. As I now realize, the reason these three evolved as a group was due to their similar management actions, which allowed them to be the last men standing among my diverse group of former clients.

Del Dunmire built what he described as a basic company. His primary mission, both defensively and offensively, was survival. He adhered to a cycle economy theory in which the experience of recessions, depressions, or unforeseen setbacks was only a matter of time. He had no debt. He not only could survive the effect of an economic downturn but also could acquire assets at bargain prices. By carefully designing and developing a monopolistic market in aircraft replacement parts, Dunmire generated enormous profits that supported lavish customer entertainment and further investment opportunity.

Garry Drummond parlayed his background with interests in social, volunteer, business, and political contacts into monopolistic coal sales contracts. With revenue generated, he transformed a small regional coal company into an international leader with an outstanding staff of key employees and monumental investments in future projects.

Whereas Del Dunmire took a conservative, controlled, low-risk approach to management, Garry Drummond, with a windfall of cash flow, was willing to take bold, huge investment risks that led to huge gains and massive tangible assets. As Drummond's surface and underground mines experienced natural depletion, the company boldly established the largest underground mine in America at Shoal Creek, Alabama, and the massive La Loma mine in Colombia, South America, one of the largest coal operations in the world, and four world-class country clubs in California, Florida, and Alabama.

Throughout his career, Drummond was totally involved with the leadership of the Drummond Company. He loved big projects but recognized his tendency to spread himself thinly. The company was staffed heavily with financial and engineering specialists, and he had take-charge leaders like Don Baxter and Charles Adair in key management positions.

Dave Noble was in a competitive business but lacking the monopolistic cash flow that blessed both Growth Industries and the Drummond Company. He was a dominating force that personally raised venture capital and who spent it wisely on reduced operations functions and salaries in order to establish competitive contracts with sales agents and to hire outside consultants to provide technical support in financial, actuarial, and HR areas.

Noble made it a point to understand everything going on in his organization. He understood the value of providing service to customers and winning the support of national sales managers. Key executives like Jack Schroeder would routinely call on and entertain agents in the field. The annual excursions for top producers and their significant others to international resorts were always attended by Noble's key managers and their spouses. Relations were cemented, resulting in semi-monopolistic relationships with many of the agents.

After struggling for years to raise working capital, the opportunity arose to form American Equity. Noble's reputation was solidified to a point at which financing was arranged almost instantaneously.

A Working Model

Anyone interested in describing what it takes to become a successful manager needs to go no further than highlighting the characteristics that I saw demonstrated by Del Dunmire, Garry Drummond, and Dave Noble. Each was in a totally different business. Each acquired working capital in different ways. Everything else was the same: They were dominating leaders, clearly in control of their companies and committed totally to their companies. They had a clear picture of areas of accountability and were quick to identify problems. Bureaucracies were stifled by open communication. Unexpected surprises were minimized. Each sought to capitalize on technology in their product or services. Each tried to create quality products, services, and relationships that could result in monopolistic or quasi-monopolistic relationships or prices enhanced by strategic sales efforts. They thoroughly understood their markets and established close personal relationships with their customers. They all valued the contributions of outside consultants, including suggestions for change.

CHAPTER TWO

CONGLOMERATES: ITT CORPORATION AND COLT INDUSTRIES

A lthough most of my early clients represented small companies and businesses, I also became a consultant to two of the most successful multiple company corporations (conglomerates) in history—ITT Corporation under Harold Geneen and Colt Industries under George Strichman.

Harold Geneen was recognized as the "father" of the conglomerate movement, popular in the mid-twentieth century, in which firms sought to acquire unrelated companies whose products and services might better withstand economic slowdowns. The key to the success of a conglomerate was management (i.e., the ability to control multiple diversified companies). Harold Geneen was the genius who put together a management structure that allowed ITT to control over 300 companies with amazing results.

Colt Industries was a conglomerate formed by key managers from ITT who focused specifically on acquiring and managing industrial companies. I consulted with both companies for over twenty years.

By the late twentieth century, global competition created situations favoring industry consolidations and mergers among large corporations in such fields as banking, retail, entertainment, automotive, and the exploding technical start-ups. Both ITT and Colt Industries divested their corporate holdings to great profits for their executives and stockholders.

Although most conglomerates are gone, what is not gone is the amazing system of management control exercised by ITT and Colt Industries. The systems worked for conglomerates. They are just as effective applied to the massive multidivisional companies operating globally today.

Andrew C. Hilton, Colt Industries/ International Telephone & Telegraph Corporation (ITT)

Andrew C. Hilton is a psychologist. He received a Ph.D. in industrial psychology from Case Western University in 1956. He worked as the director of personnel management under Harold Geneen at Raytheon and moved to International Telephone & Telegraph Corporation when Harold Geneen became president and chief executive in 1959.

In 1963, Hilton joined Fairbanks Whitney as senior vice president of administration under George Strichman, who left a management position at ITT to become president and chairman of Fairbanks Whitney, a conglomerate that had gone through a decade of mismanagement. Colt Firearms was one of its most recognized successful divisions. The Fairbanks Whitney name was changed to Colt Industries.

I was hired as a consultant to Colt Industries by Hilton and reported to him. Through my relationship with Colt, I also became a consultant to ITT. For a period of over twenty years, I had the pleasure of serving as a psychological consultant and assessment psychologist for ITT and Colt. Both companies were essentially holding companies, with ITT owning at one time over 300 diverse companies and Colt owning over fifty industrial companies. Both ITT and Colt have been restructured dramatically, and neither company exists today under its former name or organizational structure. Most former companies were reorganized to further stockholder value at a time after their long-standing CEOs had left.

Colt Industries, like ITT, was a multiple-corporation or conglomerate. Strichman was a graduate of the Rensselaer Polytechnic Institute and spent eleven years as an engineer and manufacturing executive at General Electric. From 1948 to 1958, he was director of manufacturing at the Raytheon Corporation, under Geneen. From 1959 to 1962, he again was under Geneen as president of ITT Kellogg.

Both companies were similar in structure, and both are presented as a model for all multicompany organizations to follow.

Harold Geneen, ITT

A controversial businessman, Geneen was heralded as the architect who invented the international conglomerate, acquiring over 300 companies. He was an accountant by training but gravitated into operations management at Raytheon. His *New York Times* obituary described him "as a great leader, but an autocrat often compared to Gen. George S. Patton, Alexander the Great, and Napoleon." Geneen was controversial, but his supporters would be more likely to describe him as Vince Lombardi—tough but always in the trenches with his troops. The *Times* goes on to report that "Mr. Geneen stretched his people and his company to the legal limit, scarring the company image to the point of

symbolizing arrogance and insensitivity." Like Lombardi, however, his
record stands for itself.

Geneen had an effective but often frustrating career in finance, climb-
ing the corporate ladder but lacking authority to bring about even
obvious changes. As chief financial officer at Jones & Laughlin in a
depressed steel market, his pleas for diversification were ignored. His
big break came at Raytheon, his first line position, as executive vice
president and chief of operations to long-standing president and CEO
Charles Francis Adams.

Raytheon was a technical company with outstanding engineers, growing rapidly with military contracts at multiple divisions. After surviv-
ing a power confrontation with various dissident group executives, he
restructured the organization, giving greater autonomy to each division
manager but also holding them accountable for the profit and loss record of the division.

Strategically, he avoided pitting division managers against the group
managers to whom they reported by calling for monthly meetings of
the entire top management including division managers in addition
to the regular group executives. He could thus openly discuss company plans and problems with division managers who were doing the
work and aware of issues. Geneen's famous no-surprises management
approach was initiated by his one-team system of sharing planning and
operating information (i.e., keeping everyone on the same page).

Geneen also maximized available staff resources. He leaned heavily on
two creative staff members who contributed to his success at Raytheon
and who were instrumental in his future success at ITT: Dr. Andrew

Hilton, director of personnel management, and David Margolis, chief financial officer.

Success came quickly at Raytheon. With organizational issues resolved, the talented engineering staff produced multiple engineering accomplishments. Profit margins and stock soared.

Although he also was impressed, Adams was cool to Geneen's hopes for a shot at the presidency. Geneen was quietly seeking another job. In negotiating with the ITT board of directors, he accepted the salary offered with no contract.

When Geneen came to ITT in 1959, the company had less than $800,000 in revenue, mostly in foreign telephone business. When he retired as chief executive at the end of 1977, ITT was the eleventh largest industrial company in the United States, with more than 375,000 employees and $16.7 billion in revenue. Included in ITT's 300-plus companies were such prominent businesses as Hartford Insurance, Sheraton Hotels, and Avis Rent A Car. He was a prototypical workaholic who needed to know everything. He worked seventy to eighty hours per week, and more than 100 managers were required to provide weekly reports and detailed filings each month.

In taking over ITT, Geneen faced a gigantic task. He inherited a nondescript group of international companies, mostly in Europe, that operated autonomously and merely tolerated their corporate connection and envisioned their sister companies throughout Europe as competitors. Geneen's arduous task, central to any company with autonomous divisions, was gaining central control without stifling decentralized enthusiasm and initiative.

With international companies, the process was slow. He personally worked with each of the companies but also expanded the office of the president with corporate staff and used outside consultants. With American companies, he quickly established central controls with a matrix management structure in which the chief financial officers in all companies reported directly to the corporate financial vice president, David Margolis, while sharing all information with the company presidents. With the hiring of Andrew Hilton, he subsequently had the heads of HR in the companies report directly to Hilton, as the corporate senior vice president of administration.

The difficulty for a multicompany corporation is not in finding companies to buy, but rather in figuring out what to do with them once they are acquired. ITT treated acquired companies as independent entities, avoiding the potentially severe crises that arise when companies with dissimilar cultures are merged. ITT further tried to mitigate risk by buying only companies that were recognized leaders in their respective fields with quasi-monopolistic markets.

Geneen was a person with the courage of his convictions, and he in turn was determined to run his companies with people with "brains and courage." In setting goals, Harold Geneen was only interested in hiring the brightest and best and rewarding them accordingly. He used Hay & Associates to set up a compensation system with top salaries for executives and lucrative bonuses for meeting and exceeding financial goals. With the help of a group of consulting psychologists reporting to a corporate group of psychologists, assessments were obtained on both internal managers and candidates. A check on the quality of employee selection in the divisions was established.

Financial Controls

A financial wizard, Geneen became famous for and identified with his no-surprises approach to financial reporting. His monthly meetings with presidents of ITT companies in the boardroom in Manhattan are legion. Approximately fifty of the more than 300 presidents were called into corporate headquarters to give a management by objectives (MBO) financial briefing of the quarterly results to Geneen and to make the next quarter's forecasts. Only about fifty presidents were invited at a time because the gigantic table in the boardroom could seat only fifty people around the table, though the room also included key corporate staff.

Each president made his presentation to Geneen in the presence of the other presidents. Geneen reacted to each presentation by generating rapid-fire critical questions. His intense probing in the meetings was referred to as the Socratic Method, in which each question leads to another question.

The most critical question had to do with whether an individual president's financial projections were accurate—no surprises! It was as sinful to make more money than projected as it was to lose more money than projected. Going into the meetings, everyone was apprehensive. They knew that each financial surprise could result in an almost maniacal tirade from Geneen. Most of the presidents generally believed that Geneen's "crazy" tirades were an act, but one of my close confidants on the corporate staff told me that some on the corporate staff were not so sure it was an act. Thus, the controversy surrounding Harold Geneen.

Whether his emotions were real or an act, there is no question that Harold Geneen systematically built an amazing organization over time and with totally committed energy that could bond 300 diverse companies into a corporate structure that provided almost instantaneous reciprocal decision-making. To begin with, the office of the president consisted of a group of forty highly qualified technical analysts and advisers reviewing monthly data from companies, trying to make sure that there were no surprises.

In 1984, Geneen wrote a book, *Managing*, with Alvin Moscow.[7] In his book, he acknowledged that his goal was to build a team of like-minded, exceptional individuals. He acknowledged that some of the independent, ambitious people he wanted to run his companies didn't want to work for him. They wanted to prove themselves by making their own decisions. He made clear to candidates that within ITT's organizational structure, individual company and corporate decisions were made collectively; there were no secrets and the companies operated with the same information gathered for the corporation. Pay raises and bonuses were paid to those achieving results, not those with the ideas, and advancement was for those willing to earn it.

The concept of using corporate technical advisers was a standard practice with both ITT and Colt Industries, often to the disappointment of company presidents who wanted complete autonomy. I remember once being with George Strichman at the Fairbanks Morse plant in Kansas City, meeting with a manager of engineering who had been an acting president of the company during troubling times. Strichman was delivering a message to the manager that a staff consensus concluded that he was not ready to have the permanent job. His manager said, "Let me do it. If I fail, fire me!" Strichman said, "First of all, I don't want to fire you. You have a great future ahead of you. But I also am not willing to take the risk of losing the company." The irony of my having this memory was that a description of an event involving Harold Geneen in his book was almost identical to the event I witnessed with George Strichman.

Both ITT and Colt used the concept of a staff line manager at the company level with the important task of analyzing and reporting on product design, production, and distribution issues. Aside from identifying problems for improving efficiency, a knowledgeable line manager was similar to having a permanent teacher enlarging the scope of specialized line workers by helping them understand the interconnection of their roles.

One of the basic policies at ITT grew out of the corporate meeting with company presidents. It was discovered that 99 percent of all surprises in business are negative. Regardless of the adeptness of a management team, mistakes would be made, problems would arise, the unexpected would happen. The earlier problems were discovered and dealt with, the easier would be the solution. The following requirement to the monthly reports of presidents was set by Geneen:

> Effective immediately, I want every report specifically, directly, bluntly to state at the beginning a summary containing the following facts in this order.
>
> 1. A clear short statement of the action recommended.
> 2. A brief summary of what the problem really is.
> 3. The reasoning and the figures where necessary for clarity and perspective to understand the basis of the reasoning and judgment areas leading to this recommendation.
> 4. A brief personal statement by the writer expressing any further personal opinion, his degree of confidence and any other questions he has in this respect.

Obviously, to make this kind of direct, clear-judgment statement, one must first do hard "crisp" thinking and adequate homework. Otherwise, we will get a continuation of vague, general statements and reports which indicate no clear position, or basis for any taken by the writer. In the future, this kind of "indefinite" statement and report will be subject to review with the author, and action will be taken on this point alone.[8]

In contrast to stories only about Geneen's tirades, the general management meetings brought highly diverse people together with a highly skilled staff for monthly meetings that generally lasted ten hours. As each attendee listened and contributed to the points of view of one another over time, they became a team, each more sophisticated in his/her own knowledge of the marketplace, world economics, world trade, international law, engineering, and, more specifically, the techniques of business management.

Although he managed one of the largest, most complex organizations in the world, Harold Geneen was always focused on what he considered the basics of business. In his book, he summarized his principles of good business management in just four sentences:

You read a book from beginning to the end. You run a business the opposite way. You start with the end, and you do everything to reach it.

A company, its chief executive, and his whole management team are judged by one criterion alone—performance.

Harold Geneen truly took management by objectives seriously. Under Geneen, ITT increased its earnings year over year for fifty-eight consecutive quarters.

His management style was basic and objective: He hired the brightest and what he hoped to be the best as a start. He maintained tight, centralized financial controls, and he held face-to-face meetings of ITT's profit centers, going over operations reports and looking for inefficiencies.

I witnessed how his one-team concept affected his corporate staff. On a business trip to New York, I was invited to dinner by a friend, Jim Doucette. Jim was second in command of ITT's corporate human resources group. He asked me to meet him at ITT's corporate office at 5:30 p.m. On my arriving, Doucette informed me that something had come up and he would be delayed. Time was dragging, but Doucette periodically came to assure me that it wouldn't be much longer. Finally, as 8:00 p.m. approached, we went to dinner. Doucette explained that he was filling in for his boss, the director of HR. He further explained that Geneen was in the building, and his staff had to be available when he was in the building. I knew Geneen was a workaholic. He also created a staff of workaholics.

Although it appears that ITT was an acquisition mill, most of its energy was spent in management. In the early days, considerable time was spent in eliminating unqualified staff and replacing them with qualified and carefully screened candidates. With initial success came profitability and significant appreciation in the value of company stock. The significant growth of the company was attributed to the consistent, impressive earnings and the resulting impressive increase in the stock evaluations. The ITT plan for making acquisitions was financed with company stock and accelerated by its rising value.

Geneen's preset judgments of people were minimized. He tried to judge people at ITT by the test of performance, regardless of credentials and appearance. He characterized the run of a successful business as analogous to cooking on a primitive stove with which you must be aware of the unexpected variables.

A favorite expression of Geneen mentioned in his book is that "in the business world, everyone is paid in two coins: cash and experience. Take the experience first; the cash will come later." Consistent with his own workaholic commitment, he offered the observation that a person who works ten hours per day for a year has 20 percent more experience than a person who works only eight hours per day.

Personnel Controls

Andy Hilton, with a Ph.D. from Case Western Reserve University, provided the special ingredient that made ITT and Colt different from other multiple corporations. To control the quality of management in each of the companies, it was determined that standards had to be established that could be centrally administered and monitored. All things considered, it was also determined that an objective, professional psychological assessment was probably the most reliable and objective tool available that could ensure that rigorous standards of hiring and advancement were followed throughout the organization. The strategy of weakening the power of managers to make unilateral decisions about people they hire or promote, in an otherwise autonomous organization, was a bold but critical move.

Structurally, the head of corporate human resources was a psychologist with skills in research and executive selection. As ITT grew, a separate psychological group reporting to the vice president of human resources was formed. A matrix organizational structure was established in each of the various companies, in which the head of HR reported to both the president of the individual company as well as the corporate head of human resources. Assured of the competence of their internal psychology staffs, both ITT and Colt followed similar procedures in developing their programs:

- Initially, certain a priori criteria were developed concerning the personal, interpersonal, and cognitive behavioral attributes expected of managers and professional staff within the organization.
- A diverse battery of psychological tests—including a broad selection of intellectual and problem-solving tasks, personality measures, and projective tests—was selected to measure desired characteristics. Normative data were collected on each measure from a large sample of executive and midlevel employees.
- A group of carefully screened consulting psychologists in designated areas of the country was selected to serve as assessors for the corporation to assess all management candidates and management employees. The psychologists interviewed each candidate. As part of the assessment process, the psychologists used the tests and norms developed for the company. As part of the assessment report, objective comparisons were made between the candidate and a representative norm group.
- The corporate psychologists reviewed all assessment reports and all hiring decisions.

The program was well conceived and professional. The tests were well established and researched for validity and reliability. A heavy emphasis was placed on candidates demonstrating diverse cognitive skills, and the norms for both executive and midlevel management were higher than the norms provided for a general population.

In the ITT structure, I served exclusively as an assessor in a central territory of five or six states contiguous to my Kansas City base. Over the years, I assessed candidates from close to ten different ITT companies, but my greatest number of assessments was with Hartford Insurance, Sheraton Hotels, and Continental Baking (Wonder Bread, Twinkies, Hostess CupCakes).

Continental had a regional office in Grandview, Missouri, that managed six or seven bakeries in the region. Unlike the model ITT created to hire the brightest and the best, the middle management of Continental Baking, including bakery managers and regional managers, consisted exclusively of men who worked their way up from being route drivers. Most were high school graduates with proven records of loyalty and commitment to hard work, but not at their best when taking tests. The ITT psychologists were flexible in understanding that you can't fit 300 diverse companies into the same mold.

George Strichman, Colt Industries/Fairbanks Morse

George Strichman was well suited for his career. He was an engineer who understood engineers and what it takes to run a manufacturing company. Unlike ITT, Colt Industries was focused on industrial manufacturing companies. The genesis of Colt Industries was the incorporation of Penn-Tech Corp in 1954. It was among the first conglomerates that grew entirely through acquisitions. It had been through a decade of mismanagement that ended in proxy fights and multimillion-dollar losses. It changed its name to Fairbanks Whitney. When George Strichman acquired the company in 1962, he described it as a "case history of catastrophe."

From its start in 1962 to its ultimate sale in 1987, Colt was successful in most cases in providing its executives and employees above-average wages, benefits, and career opportunities, and to its stockholders, significant financial rewards. Although known originally for its firearms, it became a broadly diversified, billion-dollar conglomerate with manufacturing plants in twenty-five states and several foreign countries.

My introduction to Andrew Hilton came in 1964. Colt Industries owned the Fairbanks Morse Pump Company, with divisions in Kansas City, Kansas; Pomona, California; and Beloit, Wisconsin. They decided to close the Pomona plant and consolidate the plants in Kansas City. Unfortunately, no one from Pomona was willing to transfer to Kansas City. Colt recognized they had a serious need to interview candidates to fill key management positions.

My mentor, Harvey Thomas, received a call from someone at the Colt corporate office. It was explained to Harvey that Colt had access to consulting psychologists in Chicago with whom they had worked with for years and with whom they had confidence. Colt was flying candidates to Chicago. With the hope of finding a local psychologist, they selected three out of the telephone book with the plan of having each interview a candidate and submit a report of their findings. Harvey suggested that they use me in the trial instead of him.

I don't remember the interview, but I was a seasoned professional used to writing diagnostic clinical psychology reports, and I had made the transition to writing management assessments. When the contact from New York reached me by phone, he complimented me and said that his boss, Andy Hilton, said my assessment was one of the better ones he had ever read. My relationship with Andy Hilton continued until the company was sold in 1987.

The problems at the Kansas City plant became severe with the confusion created by the merger. My role as assessor quickly became that of internal consultant to management, which broadened to include several other divisions.

My sudden immersion into a new and unfamiliar challenge was both exciting and bewildering. Fairbanks Morse made industrial and water systems pumps from design to manufacturing. It was a plant housing 300 people with a section for design engineers, order entry administration, information systems, HR, sales, a large manufacturing floor, and a foundry.

Fairbanks Morse needed key people in all categories, and I found myself interviewing people who were seeking positions in areas totally unfamiliar to me. As a technical company, many of the employees and managers had backgrounds in engineering.

Although I had met and knew engineers, I had never interviewed an engineer until I consulted with Fairbanks Morse. I interviewed both prospective outside candidates and those currently employed, discovering that engineers as a group, although intelligent, can be narrow in their perspective, often seeing issues in black-or-white terms. These were not ideal candidates for functioning in complex leadership roles.

I remember interviewing a candidate for a position of production control manager. I didn't really know much about production control, but in looking over the candidate's resume, I said, "You're not an engineer. Everyone I've interviewed so far is an engineer." With a sly grin, he said, "Maybe that's why I'm here."

My general perceptions notwithstanding, I also interviewed candidates and employees with engineering backgrounds and broad perspectives. As my sample grew, I came to identify a specific group of engineers who had trained in General Electric's (GE) engineering training program.

I discovered that promising engineers entering the GE training program were assigned routinely to non-engineering positions in such areas as human resources, sales, or accounting with a goal of broadening their management knowledge and perspective. As my time with Colt increased, I became aware of the many Colt managers who started their careers as engineers at GE. I sincerely believe that much of the success achieved by Colt Industries was due to the wisdom demonstrated by corporate HR in recruiting from GE.

In a 2019 *Wall Street Journal* article concerning Amazon's rise as a CEO incubator, Dana Martoll wrote:

> For decades, General Electric was America's breeding ground for corporate chiefs. Executives who rose through the conglomerate's ranks in its heyday and passed through its rigorous management program went on to run behemoths such as Home Depot Inc. and 3M Co.

At the time Colt was recruiting, GE was acknowledged as one of the outstanding companies in the world. In the book *Jack: Straight from the Gut* published in 2001 by Jack Welch and highlighting his twenty years at GE, he accuses the company during this same era of becoming fat and complacent with three and four levels of unneeded management. Apparently, GE's intentional loss became Colt's timely gain.

My early activity with the Fairbanks Morse plant in Kansas City was during the difficult period of confusion following the Pomona consolidation. Chaos existed in every area, and experienced leadership was simply not available. I found myself serving as a sounding board for staff feeling anxious about the confusion and uncertainty they were experiencing. A manager under pressure and exhibiting a drinking problem died under questionable circumstances with his car running in the garage with the door closed. To confound the problem, some staff from corporate were also concerned with the slow progress.

A popular theory of management known as situational leadership holds that autocratic leadership is appropriate in crisis situations in which those being led are untrained, immature, or incompetent. As the work situation becomes more stable and employees better trained and responsible, leadership that is democratic or even laissez-faire is more appropriate. The problems in Kansas City would certainly qualify as a crisis at that time.

Fairbanks Morse was founded in the 1880s and was one of the oldest companies in America. One of its primary plants was still active in Beloit, Wisconsin, but it was a large, inefficient facility with a large, antiquated foundry. The strategic move of consolidating Pomona and Kansas City was also a harbinger of Beloit's future demise. The immediate solution to the Kansas City problem was to move a long-term executive from Beloit to head up the Kansas City operation as division president.

The person in question worked his way through the union into top management. He was well known and feared by reputation throughout the company. His management style was to intimidate and create fear. One of his first actions was to question the manhood of a first-line supervisor and speculate about the feelings of the man's wife toward him.

It was a strategic move, using fear as a motivator, and performance did improve. People were working overtime, and the company's financial situation stabilized. Through reports from HR and accounting, both with accountability to corporate, the president's management style was known but not endorsed by higher corporate management.

My consulting activity was set by Hilton and coordinated by local HR. The president did not exercise control over me and ostensibly supported my activities. Privately, Andy Hilton assured me that the present situation was temporary and soon to be rectified.

With the presence of a new, enlightened president, Charles Elcock, I came to appreciate the Colt structure whereby a dictatorial president could not hide his actions from the corporate group. I also was integrated into the overall management structure, putting to use my group dynamics training, organizational development skills, and action research tools.

Charlie Elcock was one of the brightest, most congenial, and most focused operating presidents with whom I was ever associated. He quickly grasped the dynamics of his organization and was quick to zero in on problems and was supportive of staff. He saw me as an ally to gain information from and as a resource to intervene when it came to problem situations.

A description of two critical organizational development interventions follows:

1. The first was a chronic problem in the order entry area. A system ostensibly was in place in which an order moved through five departments—from order input through manufacturing to shipping. For some reason, problems always seemed to exist, but no one seemed to know why. Charlie gave me a Saturday to work on the problem.

   A meeting was held with twenty-some employees from the five departments that were involved. After a short speech about how we as a group are best equipped to research our own departments, we split into four groups with at least one member from each department in each group. Their task: define the problem.

   During the consolidation of the two divisions, there was much confusion and haste in establishing single operating systems. Within a few hours, the groups were able to identify numerous issues. Although each department had established its own system, there apparently had not been an overall coordinated system. As the group members shared information about their departments, it became clear that the system had problems. Several departments reported that ad hoc actions were often required to complete the order.

   The groups were so excited by their success in identifying the problem that they were ready for the next phase: solve the problem.

   They reformed into a single group and kept working through lunch. They came up with a general plan of action that included having more meetings over the next several weeks. They ultimately arrived at a permanent solution.

2. The second problem Charlie asked me to address involved manufacturing foremen who were responsible for management efficiency, which he said was measured by production hours and production costs. He showed me a chart in which management efficiency had dropped to a point at which the company would be out of business in a year if the problem were not rectified. He asked if I could interview the four foremen who were responsible for management efficiency on their respective shifts. After extensive individual interviewing of those four foremen, I could come up with only one possible issue: A new manufacturing manager had been hired approximately two months prior to my interviews. He observed that each foreman was submitting monthly management efficiency data. He informed them that they no longer needed to submit individual reports, but rather they could combine data and file one report.

When I informed Charlie, he practically jumped out of his chair and he yelled, "That's it!" He explained that the manufacturing manager relieved each of the foremen from individual accountability. To maintain high productivity and low cost, the foreman's role is that of a "heavy." If production is down, he lays off people or sends them home for a day. He is responsible every minute of his shift for seeing that production is maximized, and that cost is minimized.

Once the old management efficiency system was back in place, the crisis passed. Harvey Thomas told me that I would learn from the people I was helping. I certainly learned a lesson about the value of personal accountability in business that has stayed with me through the years.

The concept of the multiple corporation is well established in America. Of large corporations, rare are those that are not true conglomerates. Their organizational structures are similar. A small corporate staff controls a group of decentralized companies, each with considerable latitude to set its own goals and directions. These companies can be similar in composition or they can be diverse. Colt Industries, as mentioned previously, consisted of industrial companies with a strong engineering orientation. ITT was a true conglomerate, consisting of such varied companies as Sheraton Hotels, Continental Baking, and Hartford Insurance.

The Colt organizational structure, without a Harold Geneen at the helm and a smaller corporate staff, was built around a group of company presidents in related industries reporting to a technically proficient group vice president, with support from Dave Margolis, the corporate vice president of accounting.

Colt Industries, with fewer financial resources than ITT, tried to buy aggressive, growth-oriented companies that were number two or three in their respective fields but with the potential to be number one. With the addition of Andy Hilton, my primary role was greatly enlarged to provide consultation to managers in selected companies.

Two acquisitions with which I was involved offered particularly interesting challenges: Central Moloney Electric and Menasco Engineering.

Central Moloney Electric
Moloney Electric was founded in St. Louis, Missouri, in 1898 and owned primarily by the Moloney family. It grew quickly to become the

largest exclusive manufacturer of large electrical power transformers in the United States. Moloney built a new, two-story manufacturing facility on the northwest side of St. Louis with acres of land for future expansion. The top floor was designed to have all drafting, technical support, and manufacturing together.

Shortly after the turn of the century, there were three major electrical companies in the United States—General Electric, Westinghouse, and Moloney. We know what happened to GE and Westinghouse. The Moloneys lived well as a family, but they did not invest in their company. Thomas Moloney built a mansion that is still a tourist showplace. A financial windfall for the company was selling to General Motors the land adjacent to the plant to build its large St. Louis assembly plant, halting plans for Moloney expansion in the future.

In 1952, Ralph Mitchell, the city manager of Pine Bluff, Arkansas, bought the majority interest in a welding company that also built electrical distribution transformers, which fit on telephone poles and were sold primarily to municipalities. His motives were both entrepreneurial and philanthropic, hoping to stimulate the local economy. The new company was called Central Transformer Company. To promote both the company and Pine Bluff, the owner hit on the idea of inviting the chief executives of departments that purchased transformers to an annual duck shoot during the one-month season:

- Comfortable facilities were built.
- Guns, ammunition, dogs, and human retrievers were arranged.
- A French chef with access to the finest food available was retained along with young, energetic servers.
- There was no limit on liquor to suit all tastes.
- Each guest left with a box of iced ducks.

Executives were scheduled in groups for three days of expense-paid hunting, which meant that Central Transformer executives spent a solid month with limited sleep, entertaining ten different groups of prospective customers. The company grew like wildfire.

Moloney, in the meantime, continued its decline and decided to diversify into pole transformers by making an offer to buy Central. Rather than accept Moloney's offer, Central bought Moloney in 1965, creating Central Moloney Transformer Company. Colt bought Central Moloney in 1968. I worked closely with both companies and the founder and his son, who served respectively as corporate president and vice president. Neither were "business" people, and both looked forward to and profited from the guidance provided by Colt.

Central continued to grow, to enhance earnings for itself and Colt and enhance the stature and wealth of its Pine Bluff employees. In 1998, Central converted into a 100 percent ESOP. Still headquartered in Pine Bluff, Central Moloney today is a diversified electrical company. The problems at Moloney, combined with significant cost cutting from the Japanese, forced the close of the St. Louis plant and the demise of the manufacturing of large electrical transformers.

As a case study, Moloney is a company that changed little from its inception. Although its product was a leader, it didn't invest in new technology, instead sticking with the "technology" of forty draftsmen who were responsible for individualizing orders. With its second-story manufacturing floor, even a change in layout was limited.

Menasco Corporation

Menasco was an ideal company for Colt to acquire but also a company that provided personal growth opportunities for its employees and psychic rewards for its consulting psychologist. Menasco, founded by Albert Menasco in 1926, was a subcontractor that made landing gear for all major airplane manufacturers in North America. It was one of two landing gear manufacturers; the other was Cleveland Pneumatic.

The company consisted of a corporate office in Burbank, California, and three manufacturing facilities in Burbank; Euless, Texas; and Montreal, Quebec (later mover to Oakville, Ontario).

When I first interviewed a marketing representative in the Burbank plant, I was shocked to find that he was the only marketing representative. He explained that the airplane manufacturers only used Menasco and Cleveland Pneumatic and that they balanced jobs to ensure that each company received approximately the same amount of business. The companies controlled their landing gear costs without opportunity for other competitors to bid. Menasco was a true monopoly!

Menasco was highly centralized, with all planning and decision-making taking place in Burbank. All plants were organized to be cookie-cutter replicas. Each plant was strictly to provide the implementation of manufacturing projects doled out from the corporate office. By the time I became involved with the company, the Burbank corporate staff had been terminated and each plant was to operate independently. Colt had, in effect, reduced the entire cost of maintaining a redundant corporate structure, and I was to become part of a team with the goal of making each individual plant an autonomous profit center.

My task was to provide psychological assessments on key management personnel in the three divisions and to work closely with Dr. Joseph Steger, an industrial psychologist hired by Colt who was responsible for enlarging management accountabilities and for establishing long-term management development opportunities in each of three divisions. Steger received a Ph.D. from Kansas State University in psychophysics and statistics in 1967, and he had worked primarily as an academician. Prior to joining Colt, he served as provost at Rensselaer Polytechnic Institute, George Strichman's alma mater. After leaving Colt, he served as the president of the University of Cincinnati from 1984 to 2003.

The project was challenging and rewarding, and Joe and I quickly bonded as associates and friends. Each of my assessments was of critical importance to the person I assessed because he or she was confronted with a new job description, and my feedback had immediate relevance. Each president in turn was expected to work closely in the development of his staff, and I became a resource in helping them to better understand their staffs.

The following excerpts of a memo I wrote to Steger highlight my findings and activity after I had completed assessments on fifteen of the staff at one of the divisions:

> As a group, the Menasco staff is hard working and committed. They work long hours, and there is considerable peer pressure to keep on top of projects and assignments. In fact, several of the group expressed ambivalence about moving into higher-level positions because of the heavy time demand . . . By broader management standards, the Menasco group is not impressive. Most have been with the company for a long time and have learned specific rather than broad management functions. The educational level generally is low, and examples of managers seeking to further their careers by seeking advanced degrees or evening courses are nonexistent.

Jim [the president] is very hard working, task oriented, and loyal to his people. With his engineering background, he has tried to shift from being technically oriented to being more interpersonally oriented, but he has difficulty dealing with subjective aspects of behavior.

My experience with him over three visits is positive. Although he initially did not see many of the shortcomings I described in his people, he was not defensive in discussing my views, and he generally could accept the rational I presented. On the day of my final visit, we spent considerable time together discussing each of his people and exploring differential management and supervisory strategies he could use in working with various individuals. He acknowledged a need for training and broadening among his staff.

In summary, Menasco was a unique and satisfying experience. The outcome was successful: Colt Industries demonstrated its vision and capability, the employees all profited from the experience, and I felt personal satisfaction.

Although the term *conglomerate* triggers a pejorative image to many executives, I cannot think of a more important contribution to modern management than the matrix management model crafted by ITT and Colt Industries to establish unequivocal financial and HR direction along with group oversight of their individual presidents and companies. Harold Geneen was committed totally to no surprises, and he was unwilling to risk what he couldn't control, including the hiring of individuals who would not or could not accept being held accountable.

Andy Hilton was a person I admired and respected, who had enhanced my personal development by the confidence he showed in me. During the hectic period with Fairbanks Morse, he educated me about corporate management in general and about the specific strategies of Colt Industries.

After almost fifty years, the lesson I learned from Charlie Elcock about the importance of establishing and maintaining accountabilities in management is still with me. It is so difficult to hold others accountable and so easy to rationalize one's actions.

Comments

Harold Geneen had one major objective: performance.

Although he is famous for his one-team concept and his no-surprises methodology, his equal accomplishments resulted from his institutionalizing effective standard operating procedures created by his outstanding staff, including Andy Hilton and Dave Margolis (who both joined George Strichman at Colt Industries). These same procedures were established in the ITT/Colt Industries operating model that follows.

ITT/Colt Industries Management Model

1. Office of the president was established: With a tightly controlled central organization, extensive information from the companies was required and serviced by a large staff assigned to the "office of the president."

2. A Management by Objectives system was initiated: With Geneen's no-surprises mantra, MBO played a central role in forcing critical planning by company presidents.

3. A corporate psychology function, as part of HR, provided research on management effectiveness, internal psychological assessments, and oversight on assessments provided by contract assessors in the field. All external assessors reported to the corporate psychology function. The source of hiring the "best and the brightest" was a massive undertaking created by Andy Hilton.

4. Matrix management systems were established in which the heads of company accounting and HR departments reported to both the company presidents and to the respective corporate heads of accounting and HR.

5. All Colt Industries presidents reported to group vice presidents. Each group provided related products or services with which a group vice president had experience or familiarity.

6. All manufacturing companies had staff line managers. They reported directly to the vice president of manufacturing, with responsibility for oversight and consultation with all production functions from design to shipping.

In a previous section of this memoir, Peter Drucker identifies the tremendous risks entrepreneurs take in starting an enterprise. He listed five broad needs for the survival of a business enterprise, but I noted that he doesn't offer any specific examples of what an entrepreneur can do to prepare for survival. ITT and Colt Industries certainly serve as models for multicompany or multidivisional enterprises with their strongly centralized structure of control. Even with structure, both Geneen and George Strichman recognized the risk of losing a company with an inexperienced leader.

Colt Industries was a classic example showing that an ITT structure can be created without a Harold Geneen. The primary persons providing oversight to companies with related products were group vice presidents with experience in related industries such as aerospace, electronics, or steel production. Many were former engineers with GE. By restricting its acquisitions to technical companies, maintaining central control was not as complex as managing ITT. George Strichman and his successor, David Margolis, both worked closely within the system, delegating to known, experienced group vice presidents and company presidents. For example, in acquiring Crucible Steel from ITT, they also acquired the president who had an outstanding record of performance.

In Harold Geneen's book *Managing*, the first words in chapter one is the following: "Theory G: 'You cannot run a business, or anything else, on a theory.'" He goes on to talk about the management seminars he attended where he learned about Theory X and Theory Y and other theories developed by business school professors that kept him from holding himself and others accountable when he was new in management.

In the appendix on the history of behavioral management, I discuss the drive theories related to self-directed individuals—with a cautionary note. These are theories without empirical validation. They do not obviate the need for maintaining consistent systems of accountability.

There have always been great man concepts associated with outstanding leaders. Harold Geneen is regarded as such a leader. As a consultant to ITT, I was aware of his no-surprises approach to management, and I documented the outstanding organization controls established both in ITT and in Colt Industries. In reading his book, I learned about his personal philosophies, the outstanding corporate staff he directs, and the huge number of company presidents he counsels.

There is not one word about Andy Hilton's contribution in staffing 300 companies with the "best and the brightest." Nor is there a word about the matrix management structure that selects and holds accountable his outstanding staff, nor the contributions of Andy Hilton or Dave Margolis in developing the structure. Great men, apparently, don't always acknowledge the people that contribute to their greatness.

CHAPTER THREE

MULTIDIVISIONAL COMPANIES

A lthough *conglomerate* is a term not often used today, the organizational structure and practices of Colt Industries (or a similar business) should serve as a model for any company with multiple divisions.

Robert Lester, CEO/owner of the Kansas City Terminal Warehouse Company, and Joe Burstein, CEO/co-owner of Burstein-Applebee, were both successful but dominating leaders who failed to create legacies capable of perpetuating their entrepreneurial enterprises.

Hoerner Box Company and UtiliCorp United were both successful companies, but neither, during my tenure, had established predictable systems of central control over their operating divisions.

Harold Hook, whom I consulted with only at the start of his career, was an exceptional leader noted for his creativity in developing a standardized system of controls in leading American General Insurance Company to phenomenal success.

Harold S. Hook, National Fidelity Life

Harold S. Hook has one of the most impressive resumes of anyone I have ever known. In 1963, at the age of thirty-one as president of National Fidelity Life Insurance Company in Kansas City, Missouri, he was the youngest insurance company president in America. He hired me as a consultant when I was in my early thirties.

Hook was the youngest of four brothers in a family of achievers, all of whom were graduated from the University of Missouri and all of whom have had outstanding business careers. As an undergraduate, Hook served as president of the university student union. He received a master's degree in accounting in 1954. As a graduate student, he also served on the faculty of the University School of Business. He received a Naval ROTC scholarship and on receiving his commission served three years active duty on a minesweeper in the US Atlantic Fleet as an executive officer and navigator. He attributed much of his management style to the experience he gained as a naval officer.

I consulted with National Fidelity Life under Hook's leadership for about three years. We were about the same age, moved in the same social circles, and developed both a comfortable client/consultant and friend relationship. I think he offered as much advice to me as I was starting my career, as I ever offered to him.

Hook always projected an image of total competence and omniscience. His selection as president of National Fidelity Life resulted from a recommendation from Eugene Zachman, a fraternity brother at the University of Missouri to his father-in-law, the chairman of National Fidelity Life. Zachman saw firsthand the leadership Hook projected throughout his college career.

When I consulted with National Fidelity, I immediately was aware of a casual, collegial atmosphere around Hook and the people reporting to him, with Hook as the mentor. His associates were in awe of him.

I was particularly impressed in that his staff all had insurance backgrounds, while Hook became president without a history of experience in insurance.

Hook showed a keen interest in reviewing with me the reports I had written about his staff and in sharing with me his observations. He in turn shared with me his strategies and efforts to establish his presence with his associates.

In the evening when everyone left for home, Hook would visit various desks to determine the activities and projects with which his staff were involved. He would then study and brush up on the various areas in order subsequently to casually impress each individual with his relevant knowledge of their areas of responsibility. Conversely, Hook's office and desk were stark with only bare walls and a clean desk to greet visitors. There was a period when the staff took time off to study for an insurance test in a specialized area. Much to the surprise of the group, Harold showed up and, of course, aced the test.

His background in the military and the experience he gained as a commanding officer of a minesweeper had a profound impact on his philosophy and practice of management. As a commanding officer, he realized that his men would follow him to their death. If as a management leader he could engender the same type of acceptance and loyalty, he knew he could achieve impressive results.

Another thing he admired about the military was the universal clarity of commands or even expressions that had existed for generations. For example, strip-down procedures identified complex events that required a series of behaviors that all military personnel understood immediately. He recognized the value of standardizing and labeling various management practices in the way they were standardized in the military. Clarifying communication and eliminating misunderstandings was a giant step in eliminating misunderstandings among management teams.

In addition to serving as the president of National Fidelity, Hook initiated an informal management laboratory to identify and standardize various procedures and relevant information commonly applied to management. As he advanced to new career positions, he continued to add more relevant applications to his system, which he subsequently called Model-Netics.

It is interesting to note that Harold Hook's approach to standardizing management decision-making has some similarity to the no-surprises approach Harold Geneen invoked with the presidents of his ITT companies. As a preface to his system, Geneen noted that to make a direct, clear-judgment statement, one must first do hard "crisp" thinking and adequate homework. In both cases, the leaders were involved personally in the introduction of their systems, which then became standard practice in their various companies.

Harold always had a keen interest in education and teaching. His oldest brother, who had a Ph.D. in business, was a professor in the business school at the University of Arizona. My Ph.D. was the only thing I possessed that Hook coveted. He was always trying to figure out how he could squeeze in a Ph.D. on the side. Secretly, I always hoped that Hook would be awarded an honorary Ph.D. so that I could heckle him about "finally arriving."

With his reputation established, Hook left National Fidelity in 1966 to accept a position with United States Life in New York City and later was named president. Once he left National Fidelity, I lost contact with him, but I became aware of his meteoric accomplishments in business, management, and philanthropy.

In 1970, he was named president and CEO of Cal-Western States Life Insurance Company in Sacramento, California, his third presidency before the age of forty. While at Cal-Western Life, Hook was asked to join the Houston-based American General board in 1975. After gaining controlling interest in Cal-Western Life, he became the third president of American General Insurance Company (AG) in 1978. He was elected subsequently to additional positions as chairman and chief executive officer.

In addition to his management accomplishments, Hook was recognized as a management scholar and innovator, based on the structured and predictable management concepts he developed through Model-Netics. In 1971, he founded the Main Event Management Corporation (MEMC), a sales and training organization providing the structured and predictable training tools he developed through Model-Netics. The foundation program offered by MEMC through Model-Netics was touted as a management language and system of memory devices that serves as a playbook of best practices and problem-solving tools. According to Thomas D. Barlow, a longtime director, "Model-Netics is like the military with a rule and method for everything":

> Mr. Hook learned early on that what most impacts one's ability to manage and problem solve effectively is not what you know, but what you can control and use in real time. He designed Model-Netics as a management language and system of memory devices that help maximize recall of best practices for managers at all times.

In the development of Model-Netics, Harold Hook imposed his methods on virtually every area—from administration to marketing—and on the way people talk about them. The key elements of the management system are a collection of 151 buzzwords, symbols, and axioms to describe his strategies.

Learning sessions result in group understanding of each strategy and the procedure involved.

Examples of Model-Netics Strategies

Action TNT: Idea that action today—not tomorrow—is the key to high accomplishment

Attitude Stair-Steps: Concept that action to bring about a change results from a series of attitudinal changes. The five steps in the model represent awareness, understanding, concern, dissatisfaction, and action.

Procedure for Organizing Both Oral and Written Communications: General to specific, simple to complex, known to unknown

Business-Owner Concept: Idea that all managers should treat their unit of responsibility as a business within a business

Under Hook's leadership at American General, twenty-three acquisitions were completed totaling $6.5 billion as were twenty-four divestitures totaling $2 billion. Using Model-Netics as a base offering a necessary infrastructure for managing an organization, he helped to maintain a common corporate culture that proved to be critical for integrating newly acquired companies.

During his nineteen years as AG chairman and CEO, assets increased from $6 billion to $66 billion, shareholder equity grew from $916 million to $5.6 billion, market capitalization increased from $768 million to $8.5 billion, and total annuitized returns equaled 20 percent.

Aside from his outstanding business career, he served in leadership positions in more than twenty civic and philanthropic organizations. Among his many philanthropic endeavors were the establishment and annual funding for the Hook Center for Educational Leadership and District Renewal and the Joanne H. Hook Dean's Chair in Educational Renewal at the University of Missouri School of Education, the college's largest single gift.

Hook was the recipient of numerous honors and awards. In addition, he served as a member of the board of directors for numerous New York Stock Exchange companies including Chase Manhattan Bank, Continental Airlines, Cooper Industries, Inc., Duke Energy Corporation, Panhandle Eastern Corporation, Sprint Corporation, and Texas Commerce Bancshares.

He retired in 1997, but he maintained an active role in board activity and philanthropy. Two organizations that had a major impact in his life were the University of Missouri and his college fraternity, Beta Theta Pi, in which he served as president. In addition to his substantial philanthropic contributions, he devoted an amazing amount of personal time in undertaking multiple tasks in the development and operation of the Hook Center for Educational Leadership and as a regional director of Beta Theta Pi chapters, providing oversight and consultation to specific groups of chapters.

Although he had not formalized his idea of Model-Netics when I was his consultant, he was already experimenting with various models. He was intent on defining management situations that communicated immediately to a real event. He already was using an example that he used subsequently to introducing the concept of Model-Netics. The example was, "This train's going to Chicago." The message was that everyone in the group had already agreed on a plan of action. If you do not agree with the group, get off the train!

Although I have never been involved with Model-Netics, the concept was obviously highly successful for Harold Hook and his followers. Harold Geneen is regarded as one of the most effective corporate executives of all time. As I previously explained, I see similarities between Harold Geneen and Harold Hook in their specific involvement in providing meaningful decision-making strategies in the development of their executives.

Not unlike Harold Geneen, a forceful, demanding leader who achieved outstanding results with his management system, Harold Hook was a forceful, congenial leader who also achieved outstanding results with his management system. The key words are forceful and system.

In preparation for this memoir, I had hoped to have a personal meeting with Harold to have a more in-depth perspective on his professional career. He died in January 2018.

Robert R. Lester, Kansas City Terminal Warehouse Company, Inc.

In the summer of 1975, Guy McGruder, a lawyer friend of mine, asked if I would be interested in working with a long-term client with a reorganizational problem. I met Robert R. Lester, a gentleman in his late seventies, for lunch at the Kansas City Club. Lester (who always referred to others formally as Mr., Mrs., or Miss) was the sole owner of the Kansas City Warehouse Company and its subsidiary trucking firm, Terminal Transit.

Kansas City at the time had a few company headquarters, such as Hallmark Cards and the Business Men's Assurance Company, but it was primarily a major distribution center with numerous warehouses responsible for servicing a wide central section of the country. The son in a prominent Kansas City family, Lester was a Princeton graduate, an outstanding student, and a swim team letterman. Following his graduation from Princeton, he worked in his wife's family bank until the bank failed during the start of the Great Depression in 1929. He then was instrumental in converting his family-owned grocery store company into commercial warehouses in which major manufacturers could warehouse items to be distributed in the region through the transit system coordinated by the Kansas City Warehouse Company.

For most of his career he managed the operation as president and chairman, creating a near monopoly in which multiple warehouses were owned by the company with long-term contracts to house and distribute products from major manufacturers such as Libby's foods. In my initial report to Lester, I described the management climate as follows:

> Mr. Lester is a dominant figure who has and who can run the company. By experience he knows that he cannot pull out totally without having dramatic difficulties within the company. Realistically, however, he knows that he must disengage.

Mr. Lester lacks confidence in his top management group. Mr. H [his son-in-law in his mid-forties], Vice President of Sales, is seen as being poorly organized and erratic; Mr. K, Vice President of Operations, is seen as poorly organized and stubborn; Mr. C, Controller, is seen as weak and timid; and Mr. G, Director of Human Resources and Industrial Relations, is seen as abrasive and non-people oriented.

Although always polite and respectful in his dealings with subordinates, Lester believed in a top-down management structure in which one person directed the efforts of each individual manager. That individual, of course, was Lester, and Lester wanted me to help him identify or find that one individual who could replace him. As I interviewed various individuals, I discovered that interaction between departments was minimal. Each key person carried out his or her functional responsibility as defined by Lester. There was little enthusiasm for group meetings; Lester dominated the meetings, and any action plans came directly from him.

As I interviewed various managers and supervisors, I came to realize that the company was highly structured and predictable. The primary service was provided by the warehouse staffs who implemented systems that had been in place for a generation. The key positions were those of warehouse superintendents, who functioned more like foremen who stayed on the warehouse floors most of the time and who were meticulous, detail-minded, and adept at implementing existing systems. Historically, most superintendents learned their positions over several years through specific on-the-job learning experiences. Each superintendent would also have worked in multiple locations thereby standardizing procedures in each location, ensuring excellent customer service.

I came to realize that with his intelligence and Princeton education, Robert Lester was running a company designed for human engineering. The Kansas City Terminal Warehouse Company (KCTW) was being run exactly the way Frederick Taylor recommended in his book on scientific management written in 1911![9]

Notwithstanding Lester's criticism of his top staff, each was making significant contributions in their respective roles. H, though lacking in business acumen, was doing a competent job in his sales management role. K, though frustrated and often at odds with Lester, was a knowledgeable, intelligent, dedicated person looking to expand his role. He provided both support and direction to H, and I felt that he had growth potential. C was competent and cooperative, but not a forceful controller.

G, though generally reviled by his associates, was unilaterally a major factor in the success of the company. He was acquainted with all facets of the organization. He was the company "heavy," identified as being close to Lester and quick to confront others with their inefficiencies. Lester used G both as a foil and as a scapegoat. He was disliked generally and not recognized for his contributions. Perhaps one of his most impressive accomplishments was in maintaining an excellent working relationship with the Teamsters Union, who provided cartage services through the years.

With its multiple warehouse ownerships and established success, KCTW posed a formidable barrier to future competition. Although successful, the company had inefficiencies. With the narrow scope of superintendent's responsibilities, communication between functions was a serious problem in dealing with unforeseen difficulties with little opportunity to learn or develop new procedures. Problems were solved mostly on an ad hoc basis or forgotten.

In my interviews with employees, specific problems emerged, mostly related to the one-man leadership that had prevailed for so many years. Specific issues included such things as

- Inadequate customer liaison with the warehouse
- Lack of daily, weekly, and long-range communications within all departments
- Lack of a continuous program to upgrade skills and knowledge of employees
- The controller's function was underutilized
- Office systems were inadequate
- Lack of feedback over the performance of sales and operations
- Lack of meaningful statistical information to management
- Major personnel consolidation and changes needed to be made
- Too many decisions were made unilaterally by the chairman or by individuals with delegated responsibilities

From the start of my engagement, Lester gave me carte blanche latitude to interview whom I chose and to explore any issues. We had several meetings to discuss in detail my various conclusions. Although I did not challenge his philosophies of management, I knew that he initially saw that his main challenge was to find the one person who could perpetuate his model. I also realized that his disengagement from the company was a necessary action already indicated in his diminished involvement in the company and in his need for a midday nap.

In my summary report, I made the following observation:

No one person in the organization outside of Mr. Lester has the capability at present to head up the company. Three of the choices open to Mr. Lester are to continue running the company himself, to bring in a new president, or to try to strengthen the present management team until Mr. Lester can gradually disengage.

Assuming the latter approach, I suggested an office of the president with the vice president of sales and the vice president of operations sharing the office with the chairman and heading a democratic executive committee structure in which the plans and goals would be initiated by group consensus. Such a group process would also have the effect of bringing problems into the open and of opening communication processes:

> Each member of the management group should commit himself to written goals and plans concerning the implementation of his responsibilities, subject to approval by the Office of the President members. These goals and plans will be acknowledged by all group members and each group member is subject to accountability to every other member of the management group. Plans will be developed in weekly progress, planning, and communication meetings.

The report was not a total surprise to Lester, since I had been introducing the concept in our private meetings. He needed time to discuss ideas with both H and K. He agreed to go forward with the plan of shared accountability, and I sat in on several group planning and information meetings.

During the period that led up to the report, Lester's health was failing. An active horseman, he fell from a horse while vacationing in Colorado, reducing the time he spent with the company. Although both H and G assumed greater roles, I did not have further formal contact with the company. From my friend Guy McGruder, I learned that Lester had returned with a limited role.

In 1979, at the age of 84, Lester sold the company to Space Center, Inc. of St. Paul. He died in 1997 at the age of 103.

Richard Hoerner, The Hoerner Box Company

My introduction to psychological consulting to management came with a part-time position as an associate in 1959 with Ralph Ogan and Harvey Thomas in their newly formed company, Ogan, Thomas and Associates, Inc. Thomas had worked as Ogan's associate for three or four years prior to the consolidation.

Ogan earned a Ph.D. from the University of Chicago. He was in his early sixties; about six feet, three inches; and 300 pounds, usually dressed in a tailored suit that did nothing to hide his girth. He was an imposing figure—not from his size but from his loud voice and loquacious demeanor. He was friendly, positive, and persuasive but not always sensitive to the needs of others. Thomas told me about a time when he and Ogan were making a sales call to an executive who had just gotten word of a significant move in the company's stock and was trying to interrupt Ogan's discourse, to no avail.

Thomas was graduated from William Jewell College, a small Baptist college in Liberty, Missouri. He received his Ph.D. in general psychology from Washington University in St. Louis, then returned to William Jewell to head the psychology department. Thomas was extremely in-

telligent, articulate, calm, and empathic. He was active in the church
and the community and was liked and respected wherever he went.

I think he started with Ogan as I did as a part-timer, but when I met
him, he had a full schedule of clients. When I passed my psychological
assessment given by Thomas, I assumed that I would be working with
Thomas. Instead, I worked with Ralph Ogan. He had recently been
working with a new client, the Hoerner Box Company, a large private company headquartered in Keokuk, Iowa, along the Mississippi
River about 180 miles upstream from St. Louis, with multiple plants
in surrounding states. Ogan was working closely with Richard (Dick)
Hoerner, the president, chairman, and principal owner, and with the
corporate group; I was to work with the plants.

Hoerner Box had a working relationship with the Waldorf Paper
Company, one of the largest paper companies in America, and they
also—together—owned a paper mill in Idaho. Hoerner Box had two
plants producing corrugated box cardboard sheets and multiple plants
producing just cardboard sheets. Hoerner made both large and small
specifically designed corrugated and sheet shipping boxes that fit the
contour of the item shipped. The sales/marketing involved special design functions that required artistic layout and careful production coordination.

Dick Hoerner was in his mid-sixties. He was not the founder of the
company, but he inherited it from his father-in-law. He was instrumental in its expansion and in negotiations with Waldorf. His interest
focused mainly on the sales efforts, and he had excellent senior executives in corporate finance and administration who operated the corporate group. The group was strongly supportive in the hiring of Ogan,
Thomas as consultants to the company.

Although Dick Hoerner assumed presidential authority, he was involved primarily with watching the performance in sales and in keeping up to date on some philanthropic activities. He believed strongly in money as a motivator for his sales force. His salesmen were all paid a yearly salary without a formal bonus plan, except for a discretionary bonus that could be granted at the end of the year.

For the three previous years that the discretionary plan was in place, large bonuses—in one case amounting to 100 percent of salary—were awarded to all salesmen in the company. The salesmen, of course, were ecstatic, but they lived frugally until the end of the year. This was my first hint that I could find other surprises in the company. In interviews I had with salesmen, I learned they were not happy with the system.

My first assignment for Hoerner Box was visiting a corrugating plant in Sand Springs, Oklahoma. The Hoerner plants had a general manager, a plant superintendent in charge of operations with supervisors reporting to him, an office manager, an art director, one or two salesmen, and often a sales trainee. I was naive, but I met and interviewed six or seven key people and learned what I could about the operation. As a matter of principle, my interviews were directed solely at collecting information about the person I was interviewing and never asking him or her about coworkers. At the same time, after interviewing multiple employees, certain patterns emerged about the organization.

When I returned to Kansas City, I dictated my first report, hastily, and asked our secretary Carol to give it to Ogan. It came back criticized for sloppiness. It was one-trial learning for me. In addition to submitting my interview reports, I had made a personal, informal written appraisal of the operation, things that I would normally discuss with a colleague, and had it delivered as a confidential memo to Ogan. It was about three pages long and included several glaring issues and problems.

After my first trip, I could work out a schedule. There were trips planned to Little Rock, Arkansas; Tupelo, Mississippi; Fort Worth, Texas; Sioux Falls, South Dakota; and Des Moines, Iowa. Also, I needed to return to each plant to do further assessments and to provide feedbacks to individuals I had assessed previously. After making several trips and following my standard office procedure of writing my assessment reports and sending a memo to Ogan, I was informed by Ogan that the confidential reports I wrote were anticipated eagerly by Dick Hoerner and his corporate staff.

Hoerner Box was a decentralized organization but without a group vice president to monitor and direct the divisions. Through the years, inefficiencies had evolved. My reports to Ogan were the first clear observations that had been made in years. Ralph commended me and suggested that I start consulting directly to the corporate staff in Keokuk. I was excited with my assignment and recognized that with greater centralized control over the plants, I might have opportunities for initiating organizational development programs.

Less than a year after joining Ogan, Thomas, Harvey Thomas informed me that he was breaking away from Ralph and that he would like me to join him. He said he would help me recruit clients and let me keep most of my fees except for overhead, which would be minimal since we would be operating out of our homes. It was a difficult choice, but I only joined the firm because of Thomas's presence. After leaving, I realized how much I missed the latitude and comradery I enjoyed at Hoerner Box.

It was serendipitous that my first assignment was with a company in which my efforts were so highly valued simply because of management's disorganization. I anticipated involvement in meaningful organizational development projects with Hoerner Box. Most of my future clients, I came to realize, were keenly interested in the management development aspect of my role but not so interested in seeing organizational change.

Hoerner Box merged with Waldorf in the mid-1960s. Subsequently, Waldorf and Champion ended up in a proxy battle won by Champion. What followed were leveraged buyouts and lawsuits.

In retrospect, I realize that Hoerner Box Company was a good company, looking to improve, that could have been an outstanding company. Dick Hoerner, with encouragement from his corporate staff, placed considerable faith in Ralph Ogan. Ogan, in turn, placed faith in me to provide organizational feedback.

The feedback was well received, both by Dick Hoerner and the corporate management group. At the time of my leaving, a corporate discussion had been made about exercising greater central control of the divisions, but I did not learn the outcome.

Joe Burstein, Burstein-Applebee Company

Most of my client companies were successful companies seeking my services for the long-term development of managers. There were two exceptions that were failing and looking for help to survive:

1. Jim O'Crowley of Coalter Investment had me interview management personnel employed by the sporting goods chain he was managing prior to its dissolution.
2. The other company was Burstein-Applebee (B-A).

Joe Burstein and Merle Applebee started a business in 1927 selling electronic parts from the trunk of a car to amateur ham radio enthusiasts. Moving first into the basement of a drugstore, they eventually built a corporation and catalog warehouse in Kansas City, Missouri, with over thirty-nine stores throughout the Midwest, Texas, and the Rockies. Their slogan was "Everything in Electronics," and they were the forerunner of copycat enterprises like Allied and Radio Shack. The B-A annual catalogs are still collector items on eBay.

Burstein was the guru who skillfully put the enterprise together with careful financial planning. His son, Jerome (Jerry), grew up in the business and was the president, but he lacked his father's management aptitude. Following Joe's death and a dramatic market shift away from the era of home hi-fi and radio experimentation, the company hit difficult times in the 1970s. Stores were down to about fifteen, mainly around Kansas City, Denver, and Dallas. Catalog sales had been declining for several years. Although earnings were in the red, through Joe Burstein's planning, working capital was available. The working capital was guarded over by Joe Burstein's attorney, a cagey octogenarian who headed up the most prestigious law firm in town.

I was contacted by Jerry Burstein, who heard of me through a friend. The primary need was to hire a general manager to run the company. I agreed to assess Jerry Burstein and his key managers and a prospective candidate who also was recommended by Jerry Burstein's friend. Jerry Burstein and his management staff were marginally qualified for management, but they were all long-term, dedicated employees.

The candidate was outstanding. He was in his late thirties and had spent his entire career with Sears, Roebuck and Company in an assortment of mid-management roles in both store and catalog positions. He understood the role he was to play and almost immediately transferred his Sears experience into a working model for the whole group.

A positive chemistry seemed to have permeated the group. Much was due to the confidence, patience, and direction coming from the general manager. In meeting with the lawyer, I discovered that the only reason he was releasing working capital was because he didn't trust Jerry Burstein and his group and assumed that I would be monitoring them, thus viewing me with special status.

The next few years were positive in the sense that the company was still viable, but unseen by anyone was the realization that the market was gone forever. Survival was possible only with a major shift into the coming consumer electronics chain. The general manager left after securing a job in his hometown. I also ended my relationship with the company. The lawyer recommended a friend for the general management position who had a strong background in management, but who was in his seventies. The company was sold in 1980.

In searching the Internet for this vignette, I ran across "50+ Years of Ham Radio Memories," consisting of letters from ham radio aficionados who dreamed about a trip to the B-A warehouse in Kansas City and who remembered the bargains. The highlight of a purchase seemed to be buying at the lowest cost. One letter, written by an articulate "ham," remembers buying one coil of 500 feet of #18 Copperweld wire for only $1.88.

It was a buggy whip problem. B-A was selling electronic parts. Their competitors were selling televisions.

Richard C. Green Jr., UtiliCorp United, Inc.

I started a short consulting assignment with UtiliCorp late in my career. I did not have much impact or history with UtiliCorp, but it was a fascinating company with a fascinating history.

Following his graduation from Southern Methodist University in 1976 with a BS in business with a major in accounting, Richard C. (Rick) Green joined the Missouri Public Service Company, a Kansas City public utility controlled by the Green family, providing energy service to parts of Kansas City and rural areas of Missouri. Following the death of his father in 1982, Rick Green, at the age of twenty-eight, became the fourth generation of the Green family to head the Missouri Public Service Company as president and CEO.

Demonstrating a bold entrepreneurial spirit, Green made a bid to acquire the Kansas-based Gas Service Company in 1983, but he lost. Seeking outside consulting direction, he developed a formal business plan that clearly identified the company's regulatory, weather, and general economic risks and sought to acquire strategically located energy generation and related businesses. With a plan of reorganization established, the company went public and the geographically specific name of the company was changed to UtiliCorp United, Inc. Over the next few years, UtiliCorp acquired the following companies: Peoples Natural Gas in Omaha, Northern Minnesota Utilities, West Virginia Power, West Kootenay Power and Light in British Columbia, and Michigan Gas Utilities.

UtiliCorp achieved its expansion—while avoiding a substantial increase in debt or company rates—by continually offering shares of stock for sale. Strategically, the company was seeking decentralized partners. They also sought to increase employee ownership of the company to

25 percent in the belief that it would increase employees' stake in the success of the company.

Rick Green had heard of me and invited me to meet with him. I was not looking for a new client. At the time, I was in my mid-sixties with a base of long-term clients in which I was involved with broad management issues. I also was operating as a part-time CEO of the manufacturing company I owned in California.

Green explained his goals, and we agreed to my assessing him with the immediate task of interviewing his corporate staff. Green was an outstanding person. He had a relaxed, friendly, collegial management style with a ready sense of humor. His father, whom I met once, was a serious-minded, conservative person who exercised unilateral control over all functions. The company had been more akin to a top-down, first-generation company with money in the bank and a frugal approach to risk investment. UtiliCorp looked like an interesting challenge.

Green had smarted from his early corporate confinement, reacting quickly in his new position, as shown by his calculated investment strategies and by delegating broad authority to his management staff and his corporate partners. My first task was to assess the corporate group. Most had come from Green's father's organization and provided a stable administrative structure. Rick had also added or intended to add staff to new corporate positions. His most important addition was his younger brother, Robert K. (Bob) Green, in his middle to late twenties, who had recently joined the company.

Bob Green was an intelligent person with a sound academic background in business and an active grasp of participative management concepts. He interviewed well, and I saw him as a person with excellent long-term potential.

I spent a long session with Rick Green explaining my background in working with ITT and Colt Industries. I stressed the importance of having a top professional HR manager and an experienced group vice president to impart central communication and control.

He agreed that the company needed a seasoned executive to work with Bob and that a high priority was to add a professional HR person. He had already interviewed a seasoned executive, and my highest priority was to conduct an assessment.

Due to a reorganization, the top American Telegraph and Telephone (AT&T) executive in Kansas City, Clark Redick, was available. In his late forties, with a six-foot, two-inch frame, Redick was a complete executive with professional knowledge and perceptive interpersonal skills. He was hired in a staff role to be an adviser to both Greens. The desired HR position was not filled during my tenure.

I had bonded quickly with Redick, and our views about strengths and weaknesses in the company matched. I had interviewed the top executives in the companies, except for Northern Minnesota Utilities, and found them to be mostly competent, happy with their positions, and eager to contribute.

All general managers except one had been with the acquired companies. The exception was a small West Virginia utility servicing an area around the town of Clarksburg. The company was a spin-off from Dominion Resources and had a small staff hired from the outside. It was the one company not performing up to expectation.

Redick was a strong-willed person with a fast-track history as a line manager with AT&T. He confided in me that he and Rick had philosophical differences.

Following a request from Redick, I made a consulting visit to the troubled Clarksburg company. A day or two after I had returned, l received a telephone call from Rick Green informing me that my relationship with UtiliCorp was being terminated. I had worked with UtiliCorp less than a year, and I knew that my bonds were not solidified.

I met with Rick Green for coffee the next day. He was congenial, but he did not reveal why I was being terminated. I assumed it was related to Redick sending me to Clarksburg.

Redick was also terminated shortly after the day Rick called me. He had been with UtiliCorp less than six months. Redick accepted a position in Miami with Wackenhut, the country's leading security company. We kept in touch for a while. He became president and CEO, staying with Wackenhut until he retired.

My personal relationship with UtiliCorp ended with that meeting with Rick Green. The continued history of UtiliCorp that follows was gleaned from newspaper documents. I had no personal contact with anyone in the company.

Several years after I left UtiliCorp, a small division of Northern Minnesota Utilities named Aquila, emulating Enron, turned out to become a leading wholesale energy marketer. As group vice president, Bob Green was accorded the title of COO and chairman of the Aquila subsidiary, which included operations in the United Kingdom and parts of Europe. In 2001, UtiliCorp spun off Aquila but then bought it back in 2002 and named the entire corporation Aquila, Inc.

Aquila's stock price peaked at $37.55 in May 2001 and ranked number thirty-three on the Fortune 500. The stock plummeted to $6.75 in July 2002 in the wake of the Enron scandal. The company ultimately sold assets and merged with former competitors.

Comments

Although I only consulted with Harold Hook at the beginning of his career, he was obviously an outstanding, creative, successful leader who had the ingenuity to turn a military model into a supportive, developmental training approach. Like Geneen, he was a strong leader in a structured system in which all personnel learned and used a standard management system, not unlike a military system with a revered, unquestioned leader. Like Geneen, he acquired multiple companies, standardized their procedures, and maintained central control. Like Geneen and George Strichman, he wanted executives who fit into an established, predetermined structure.

Unlike Geneen, Hook was collegial, not autocratic, in his management style. He developed a system that was not unlike the one-team concept of ITT, but the system, not Harold Hook, was the monitor.

Both the Kansas City Terminal Warehouse Company and the Hoerner Box Company were highly successful, quasi-monopolistic companies. Both had owners as CEOs who were not in tune with modern concepts of management. Both realized a need for reorganization, but my consulting relationships with both companies ended before I knew the outcome of the proposed reorganizations.

Burstein-Appleby was a pre-Depression company with a brilliant owner who structured and directed the enterprise. The model was successful, but as Del Dunmire noted, "If the customer does not need the product, the enterprise cannot succeed."

UtiliCorp United was a promising company, but I was terminated as a consultant prior to the completion of their reorganizational planning.

CHAPTER FOUR

LEGAL MONOPOLIES

The world is controlled by people who have monopolistic advantages, whether they are in special interest industries or in unions that work for them. It doesn't take much to find them. Whole countries, like Japan, are bound by such arrangements. The advantages to being part of a legal monopoly or oligopoly are incalculable. Once a monopoly is established—no matter how irrelevant its reason for existing—it may take generations before it can be broken.

A feature article in the *Wall Street Journal* described how a wholesale distributor monopoly was created in the liquor industry in 1933 following the repeal of Prohibition. Because of fear of gangster control, the US government mandated by law a three-tiered marketing structure with a wholesale distributor operating between the producer and the retailer.

Almost eighty years later, the monopoly was still flourishing. One of the major distributors, Southern Wine and Spirits of America, had revenues over $3 billion, making it bigger than some industry giants. Four other distributors had revenues over $1 billion. The wholesaler's cut typically amounts to about 18 percent to 25 percent of the price to the retailer for wine and 15 percent to 25 percent for liquor. Most of the major distributors have multiplied their growth through buying the monopolistic franchises of smaller wholesalers strategically located around the country.

The popularity and price of wine has escalated dramatically, but rewards of producers are not commensurate. The monopoly of distributors not only drains profits but also dictates what products to sell. When the wine growers tried to sell their product directly to retailers in Florida, Southern Wine and Spirits prevailed upon the legislature to change the infraction from a misdemeanor to a felony. Similar laws exist in eight states with the wholesaler lobbyists pressing for tighter legislation in all states.

Of course, there are striking examples of the government breaking up monopolies such as AT&T and the deregulation of the airlines. Although both AT&T and many major carriers were bloated and inefficient, these were not the reasons for their deregulation. The political pressure exerted by those wanting to join the oligopoly led to the assault on AT&T.

AT&T Southwestern Bell

The American Telephone and Telegraph Company (AT&T) was founded in 1885 by Alexander Graham Bell, the inventor of the telephone, and his investors. After acquiring the Bell Telephone Company, it attained monopoly status as the primary phone company in America until antitrust regulators split the company in 1982.

Harvey Thomas had an arrangement with the Southwest Research Institute (SRI) to undertake selective research projects acquired by SRI. One such project on which I collaborated was with AT&T Southwestern Bell, the largest of the "Baby Bells." The company had done a study in which it was determined that in the not-too-distant future, AT&T would need to hire every available female in America to handle operator services. A decision was made to invest heavily into technology and to evaluate the present status of female telephone operators in the company. It was the latter project to which we were assigned.

Our project took place in the city of Houston in the early 1960s. Throughout the city were satellite telephone offices with female operators handling operator assistance calls generated in their respective service areas. Each office was staffed with a head operator and a supervisory staff totally involved with the supervision of all telephone operators on three shifts, a total of approximately seventy operators.

We were responsible for visiting six different offices to interview the head operator and approximately five telephone operators at each location. Our primary contact was a vice president of HR located at the Southwestern Bell corporation office in Houston. From him we learned that in the AT&T structure, the head operator had close to dictatorial status. He had not spent much time in any of the offices and could not provide much detail. He did inform us that turnover in operators was high, and he identified turnover as a high priority he wanted us to address.

Of the six offices, five were cookie-cutter replicas, but one, Ashland, was unique. The offices had specifically defined job descriptions, and all provided extensive procedural training. A primary role of a supervisor was to informally listen in to routine calls to determine if standard protocol was being followed. Remedial feedback from supervisors was given as quickly as feasible. Calls were expected to be answered within fifteen seconds, and a technical monitoring system was in place to record each operator's performance. Although an operator never faced the public, the required dress code was full dress: no slacks, high-heeled shoes, full-length hose.

Interviews with telephone operators were surprising. Although the women disliked eavesdropping from supervisors, no one talked about quitting. Their biggest fear was about losing their jobs to circumstances beyond their control. Although the company, like all companies, acknowledged the existence of sick leave, in practice, sickness was considered an inability to do a job. Employees were terminated routinely as a forced resignation.

Incredibly, the company that was worried about high turnover was firing people who were sick enough to take sick leave! One young woman was in tears describing how she kept coming to work with measles, praying each night that she would not break out with red spots and lose her job.

Now for the unique Ashland office. Although the head operator was subject to the same guidelines as her peers, she operated in a more democratic, creative fashion. She had group meetings to discuss problems and issues. Her supervisors, rather than spending most of their time spying, spent their time in supportive relationships assisting and advising. Rather than making the fifteen-second deadline on answering calls a punitive experience, at Ashland, the subunit with the lowest time for the week was rewarded with small gifts and allowed to come to work in sloppy clothes on Friday.

The young women we interviewed knew that some women were terminated for sickness in other units, but they did not personally know any of the individuals. The head operator at Ashland stated that she did not follow any forced resignation procedures.

When we submitted our report, the HR vice president professed not to know anything about the forced resignation procedure, but he vowed to see that it was addressed. Shortly after our assignment, I terminated my relationship with Harvey Thomas to start my own consulting organization. With its monopolistic status and profitable dictatorships, I doubt that any dramatic change took place within the company.

In 1970s, the Equal Employment Opportunity Commission (EEOC) won a landmark discrimination case against AT&T and its historic settlement benefited some 15,000 women and minority Bell Operating System employees. At the same time, AT&T was the largest employer in America, with 750,000 employees. AT&T's top-level executives were all white males unfamiliar with the sting of discrimination. Of 100,000 Bell System telephone operators, only about a dozen were male. When the case settled, AT&T agreed to hire more women and more minorities into supervisory positions, hire more men into positions typically reserved for women, and ensure equal pay.

Although there were competitors, AT&T acquitted its status as a natural monopoly due to the heavy cost of providing telephone lines. AT&T increased its control of the telephone system through its leasing arrangement for telephone and telephone equipment made by its subsidiary, Western Electric. These phones were leased by customers from AT&T, generally paying many times over for their phones and connections. This monopoly made millions of extra dollars for AT&T, which had the secondary effect of greatly limiting phone choices and styles.

The AT&T monopoly was penetrated in the 1980s. The gradual rise of technology through microwave communication and fiber optics led to the antitrust suit in which AT&T agreed to divest its local exchange service operating companies in return for a chance to go into the computer business. AT&T's local operations were split into seven independent Regional Bell Operating Companies known as the Baby Bells.

Forced to compete with other manufacturers, Western Electric eventually closed its US phone manufacturing plants. AT&T, reduced in value by about 70 percent, continued to run its long-distance services through AT&T Communications, although it lost market share to competitors MCI and Sprint.

AT&T capitulated, but it did not give up easily. A sign hung in many Bell facilities in 1983 read

> There are two giant entities at work in our country, and they both have an amazing influence on our daily lives . . . one has given us radar, sonar, stereo, teletype, the transistor, hearing aids, artificial larynxes, talking movies, and the telephone. The other has given us the Civil War, the Spanish-American War, the First World War, the Second World War, the Korean War, the Vietnam War, double-digit inflation, double-digit unemployment, the Great Depression, the gasoline crisis, and the Watergate fiasco. Guess which one is now trying to tell the other one how to run its business?

I remember when the antitrust regulators were splitting AT&T into Baby Bells. One comment from a European authority appeared in the *Wall Street Journal*, noting that there was only one workable telephone system in the world and the US government was dismantling it!

I was familiar with Harold Geneen's comments about his first visit to ITT's European telephone operations.[10] Each country was still fighting World War II. No information was shared by sister companies. Instead they were treated as rivals. Worse, they designed their telephone switching and other equipment so they were not interchangeable. Each seemed satisfied with its own bureaucracies and archaic management practices.

AT&T was a powerful monopoly coining more money than some countries. Before my visit to Houston, I grudgingly paid the outrageous cost and add-on for my required rental of my telephone, but the product was indispensable, the service outstanding, and the technology coming out of Western Electric was awesome.

I had a brief look at how AT&T had abused its monopoly to enrich investors, stockholders, and executives. The bureaucracies within AT&T were so entrenched, 100,000 operators were controlled by an autonomous dictatorship with its own rules (i.e., a company within a company). What a great field for organizational psychologists, if only HR had the authority or even awareness to initiate change.

Trans World Airlines (TWA)

During my time working with Harvey Thomas in the mid-1960s, I assisted him on a project with TWA, a major airline from 1924 to 2001. Howard Hughes acquired control of TWA in 1939. Along with American, United, and Eastern, it was one of the big four domestic airlines. After World War II, he led the expansion of the airline to serve Europe, the Middle East, and Asia.

The airline had been headquartered in Kansas City but between 1954 and 1958 moved its headquarters to New York City. The servicing of the fleet was accomplished at a facility at the Kansas City International Airport. At its peak, the airline was one of Kansas City's biggest employers, with more than 20,000 employees.

Howard Hughes was one of the richest men in America, with careers as a business tycoon, record-setting pilot, engineer, aircraft designer, film director and producer, and philanthropist. Starting in the late 1920s, he produced classic movies such as *Hell's Angels* and *Scarface*. He controlled the RKO film studio. In 1932, he formed the Hughes Aircraft Company, designing unique aircraft such as the *Spruce Goose*. He personally set multiple world air speed records.

In his twenty-seven-year ownership of TWA, Howard Hughes was recognized internationally as a creative genius with multiple talents but with equally recognized eccentric behavior and a secretive, indecisive style. Consequential decisions were made laboriously on his terms. He had diverse interests, and his company involvement was sporadic and often catastrophic, a result of his penchant for making unilateral decisions. In later life, he became known for his reclusive move to Las Vegas and heavy investment into Las Vegas hotels and casinos.

Hughes relinquished power in 1961 in a financial battle that resulted in Charles C. Tillinghast, a former chairman of Bendix corporation, becoming chairman of TWA. Under a court order in 1966, Hughes was forced to sell his stock at a profit of $546 million.

Hughes was an unpredictable leader who could fly into Kansas City with a commandeered airplane full of movie stars, fire multiple people while there, and commandeer another airplane and be on his way. His airline grew not only in size but also in structure to protect itself. Fired people had new jobs in newly created departments. Every pilot had been trained in the military. The pilot's union was strong, and several top managers, including the president, were former pilots. TWA was operated much as a military organization. Orders came down from corporate, but operating people were rarely involved in planning.

Its inefficiencies notwithstanding, TWA was making money. TWA was an oligopoly. The key to its success was the government regulation of fares. Airlines could not compete on fares. Instead, airlines were known for their snacks and their gourmet service to first-class customers. Some employees with travel privileges would take a date on a nonstop trip from Kansas City to San Francisco and back merely to enjoy the amenities available to first-class passengers.

Normally, pilots make ascents and descents quickly to conserve fuel. To demonstrate their authority, on a designated day, pilots would deliberately make ascents and descents slowly to waste fuel. Flagrant abuses from the hourly union were commonplace, such as double accounting when one had two different assignments on the same day. A theft of a casket by union employees resulted in a body left on the floor of the shipping area at John F. Kennedy International.

The TWA purchasing agents buying aircraft replacement parts were under extra pressure to keep aircraft flying and generating revenue. In a previous chapter, I described how Del Dunmire created his own monopoly at Growth Industries by exploiting pressured and loosely controlled TWA purchasing agents.

TWA had a reputation for being a good technical airline but for failing in customer service. One way that management tried to solve the problem was through corporate HR coming up with a battery of unreliable personality selection tests with unrealistic standards of measuring various skills. Literally, no one could legitimately "pass" the test battery as selected and structured, and HR people around the country could only reach hiring needs by secretly falsifying scores.

The president at that time was a former pilot. Informal stories about his rudeness and inappropriate behavior were commonplace.

Charles Tillinghast sought to change the culture with the assistance of a former staff executive from Ford who became Tillinghast's representative to assist the TWA corporate group of executives to bring about constructive change. Through one of Harvey Thomas's friends, a TWA Kansas City executive, Thomas & Associates was picked to work through Tillinghast's representative with the corporate group in New York. First, we had to do our research. Thomas was to undertake the key corporate interviews, and I was to interview midlevel executives in New York and Kansas City.

On balance, the company had a core of competent, dedicated employees. The major problems were in the executive culture of a small group reporting directly to the president and the strongly independent unions representing the pilots and the hourly employees. Although ours was an ambitious project, the accomplishments were mixed.

My two main accomplishments were first, an all-day workshop on nonunion selection with approximately thirty human resource executives and staff from all offices and second, the construction of a selection test for the promotion of hourly union employees.

The workshop reviewed the problems with the existing test battery and led to a group discussion of alternative strategies. Using a questionable battery of tests was not desirable, so a model of the ideal employee was developed as a standard for collecting interview data combined with the administration of a valid measure of intellectual proficiency. It was determined that immediate selection decisions would be made by the HR interviewers but that the process would be validated longer-term by a research procedure in which personal data and additional test data were accumulated at the time of hiring.

I was not involved long enough to determine the ultimate effectiveness of the selection process, but the success of the workshop was unquestioned in terms of reducing anxiety among the HR staff. In the psychological literature of the era, a concept of mental illness known as a double bind emerged, in which a parent orders a child to perform an impossible task such as opening a locked door without a key, and then admonishing the child for failure to obey. The whole HR group had been confronted with potential double bind stress!

As we acquired data on TWA employees, we discovered that the lowest level position was one that was involved with washing and cleaning the airplanes and the highest was the position of chairman. Between these two positions were seventeen layers of management, which Tillinghast recognized as substantially too many. With resistance from the corporate staff and the unions, no reorganization was attempted during my limited tenure with the company.

Another startling statistic was the realization that the only requirement for admission to the lowest level union position was a valid driver's license and that all promotions were based solely on seniority. An entry-level employee could conceivably achieve the highest-ranked union position, responsible for the loading of baggage, which—if done incorrectly—could result in the airplane crashing.

When asked for a solution, I proposed establishing standardized intellectual and aptitude norms for each level of promotion. Entry out of the lowest position required skills of a high school freshman with a C grade point average. Skills for qualifying as a loader required intellectual and spatial aptitude skills of a high school senior with at least a B grade point average. Between the two extremes, reasonable promotion standards were set for each level of advancement.

After my developing the proposed selection system, the union filed a lawsuit that went to trial. I was not informed of the lawsuit, but Tillinghast's representative told me that the union brought a psychologist to the trial who testified that my proposed system was fair and consistent with accepted psychological practices. He further informed me that the company won the lawsuit but that the company lawyers decided not to use the system for fear of the union's reaction.

Shortly thereafter, I learned through Thomas that the management group was successful in blocking Tillinghast's strategy for change. Our contact under Tillinghast was terminated, and by association, the services of Thomas & Associates were terminated.

The ultimate demise of TWA came with its third bankruptcy, in 2002, but its fate was sealed when President Jimmy Carter signed the Airline Deregulation Act, turning what had been a controlled system of cost and profit into a flurry of desperate competition. With its inherent inefficiency, TWA could not compete and lost control to corporate raider Carl Icahn. Hemmed in by inordinately stringent long-term labor contracts, Icahn sold off its profitable overseas routes, leading to an eventual merger with American Airlines.

The major campaign for deregulation was orchestrated by Dick Ferris, the CEO of United Airlines. As the major player, United saw deregulation as an opportunity to crush competitors, like American Airlines, and new upstarts like Southwest and Texas International. United lob-

byists were largely responsible for writing the Kennedy-Cannon deregulation bill that led to the Airline Deregulation Act of 1978.

Wall Street Journal reporter Thomas Petzinger, Jr. wrote a fascinating
case study describing how American's future president, Bob Crandall,
outmaneuvered United's Dick Ferris, allowing American to achieve
its preeminence among world airlines and to make billions of dollars.
The strategy involved equipping major travel agents with American's
Sabre reservation system, manipulated so that only American's flights
received preferential listing at the top of the first computer screen.

As quoted by Thomas Petzinger, Jr.:

> Because running an airline demands a single strategic vision,
> least the delicate choreography of planes, people, timeta-
> bles, and money falter, the airline business both attracts and
> promotes executives obsessed by control. These are industry
> chieftains who flourish at the center of all decision-making,
> who love risk, who crave victory, and who are ruthlessly
> averse to defeat.[11]

In 1989 when he almost lost $358 million on an investment in US
Airways, Warren Buffet is reputed to have commented that the best
thing he could have done for airline investors was to have shot down
the Wright brothers in their Kitty Hawk flight. One hundred eighty-
three airlines have gone bankrupt since 1978.

International Business Machines (IBM)

Two former small clients, Unimark, Inc. and Marsh & McLennan
Management, are being combined here, not that they were related in
any way but because both of their founders had prior histories working
for IBM. Robert (Bob) Wagner was a former senior executive and sales

manager at IBM, a former president of Waddell & Reed, a leading Kansas City mutual fund investment company, and the founder of the management consulting group of Marsh & McLennan, a leading commercial insurance company.

Dean Lawrence was a research engineer at IBM and the founder of Unimark, Inc., a manufacturer of airline ticketing systems. At IBM, in addition to his providing technical support for the sales group, he was involved with the design of the Sabre reservation system for American Airlines. Sabre, with two IBM 7090 mainframes, was the first airline reservation system to work over phone lines.

Both Unimark, Inc. and Marsh & McLennan Management were service companies. They will be discussed in chapter five.

For over fifty years, IBM was recognized as one of most profitable, successful, and admired companies in the world. In my interviews with Wagner, Lawrence, and Del Dunmire, the philosophies and practices of IBM were discussed in detail. Dunmire was an inveterate student of IBM, modeling much of his company, Growth Industries, around IBM's sales and pricing practices. With firsthand information about IBM, I decided to include an overview of IBM management in my memoir, even though the information through me is "secondhand."

In 1915, Thomas J. Watson Sr., the former number two executive at the National Cash Register Company, became president of the Computing-Tabulating-Recording Company (CTR). In 1924, the name was changed to International Business Machines (IBM). Tom Watson was a salesman, and he quickly implemented a series of effective business tactics, including generous sales incentives, a focus on customer service, and an insistence on well-groomed, dark-suited salesmen with white dress shirts. The sales force was groomed to establish both close social relationships with customers and a professional image of competence in providing large-scale tabulating solutions for businesses, all at great cost.

The company continued to grow and to add many new products and systems applications including a rapid punch card machine, a tabulating machine, and an electronic typewriter that became one of its most widely known products. It also became a leader in creating employee satisfaction and loyalty, being one of the first major companies to introduce a forty-hour week, group life insurance and pension benefits, paid holidays and vacations, training and jobs for those with disabilities, and the adoption of equal opportunity hiring practices.

IBM was the leading provider of business services to private, government, and military customers. It also partnered with leading MIT researchers in developing military and defense computer applications for the government, thus having an inside monopoly on evolving computer technology.

Thomas J. Watson Sr. died in 1956, replaced as chief executive by his eldest son, Thomas J. Watson Jr. The younger Watson quickly created and codified a modern management structure. Included in the structure was an increase in technology research. Thus, IBM intensified with customers the image of professionality of the sales force by providing a group of "hidden" technician support/ advisers who prepped salesmen with solutions posed by client questions.

A breakthrough came in 1964 with the introduction of the revolutionary System/360 mainframe, the first large integration of a computer to use interchangeable software and peripheral equipment. IBM was in a monopolistic position, selling a bundled service in which it provided direct support and strategic relationships with data center managers in customer companies. They taught these managers how to create data processing empires, which in turn required an elaborate network of IBM equipment and services, sold also at monopolistic prices.

Del Dunmire describes Growth Industries as a marketing company modeled after IBM. He said, "We can make the finest precision parts in the world, but if we can't sell them at a worthwhile profit, we might as well close the doors." Although Bob Wagner was on a fast track, regarded as one of the top executives in the sales/marketing sphere, he described a top-down mentality that stifled innovation and that led to its failure to capitalize on its leading edge in the burgeoning personal computer movement.

He was invited to his first corporate long-range planning session in the early 1970s, chaired by Watson Jr., with a select group of senior executives who ostensibly were some of the most knowledgeable and professional individuals in America. He discovered that the planning session was really an information session explaining the specific tasks and goals expected from each divisional executive's work group. When questions were addressed to Watson, he reacted with anger and cautionary advice that group members should "just do their jobs."

Wagner, who had been approached by headhunters, moved on to head Waddell & Reed. During a period in the 1990s, anticipating layoffs, Dean Lawrence and two contemporary IBM engineers, seeing an opportunity to capitalize on their reputations, decided to assemble and sell reservation and ticketing systems to the international airline market.

The 1990s were a troubled period for IBM. With its bloated organization and failure to anticipate the market shift to personal computers, IBM took a $10 billion loss in 1992. Employment dropped over the next three years to 220,000 from 400,000. The unemployment market was saturated with former IBM salespeople. Initially, companies anticipated a windfall in available sales executives, only to discover quickly their shallow management foundation. There came a time when the mere mention of an IBM history ensured rejection.

The recovery of IBM started in 1993 with the hiring of Lewis V. Gerstner Jr. as CEO, the first CEO since 1914 who was recruited from outside the company. Gerstner had a background as a management consultant at McKinsey & Co., eleven years as a top executive with American Express, and four years as chairman and CEO with RJR Nabisco. He adopted a triage mindset, cutting expenses but saving the IBM image by integrating units and maintaining an approach to meeting customer requirements even if they were from an IBM competitor. IBM today is again considered to be one the premier international companies in the world.

When Gerstner became CEO of IBM in 1993, it was no longer a legal monopoly and had an operating loss of $10 billion. His triage task was to reduce overhead with the elimination of nonprofit and/or nonpromising companies. Investments were to go to promising tech companies and services and to support what has become the largest industrial research organization in the world.

He also tried to inculcate a participative model of communication at all company levels. In an attempt to redefine values, the company sponsored a three-day Internet conference with 50,000 employees. The mission was to discuss key business issues. The result was the identification of three key company values:

1. Dedication to every client's success
2. Innovation that matters—for our company and the world
3. Trust and personal responsibility in all relationships

The company today has a large and diverse portfolio of products and services, which fall into categories of cloud computing, cognitive computing, commerce, data and analytics, Internet of Things, IT infrastructure, mobile, and security.

The company has shown steady, even outstanding, growth from 2006 through 2014 when revenues hovered around $100 billion and net income was around $15 billion. While still profitable in 2017, the revenue was $79 billion with a net income of $5.753 billion.

Comments

AT&T was a monopoly for almost 100 years. Its management, though discriminatory, autocratic, and self-serving, was not unusual for the era in which AT&T operated. AT&T's breakup wasn't surprising once new technology companies were pushing to join the monopoly.

AT&T did not go away. The seven Baby Bells were regional amalgamations of AT&T companies throughout the country. Three of the original Bells survived with AT&T and Verizon emerging as the two largest telecommunication companies in America.

TWA's story is not so positive. TWA's fate was probably sealed when Charles Tillinghast was thwarted from instituting change, but certainly sealed with the Airline Deregulation Act of 1978. My firsthand experience watching the demise of a hometown success was a frustrating experience.

IBM's situation, like AT&T's, was inevitable and, for the most part, positive. It is still one of the largest and most successful companies in the world.

In the late 1970s, John Houseman, an octogenarian actor, made a famous, oft repeated TV commercial for the Smith Barney brokerage firm: "They make money the old-fashioned way—they earn it!" IBM is still a great company, but they are still looking to make money the old-fashioned way—through a monopoly!

CHAPTER FIVE

SERVICE COMPANIES

A s a consultant, I formed a close affinity for service-oriented companies and the people they employ. They generally were highly intelligent, broadly educated employees with natural interpersonal flexibility.

My early academic interests were in liberal arts, and I could envision myself being comfortable employed in any of the companies I describe in this chapter. As service companies, their reputations were of paramount concern, and major economic downturns and crises never seemed to be insurmountable. Most were quasi-monopolies. Companies that no longer exist were sold or merged at propitious times.

J. Kenneth Higdon, Business Men's Assurance Company (BMA)

After receiving my Ph.D. from the University of Kansas in 1959, my wife and I decided to make suburban Kansas City (Prairie Village, Kansas) our home, with the hope of building my practice as a psychological consultant to management. One of the problems that I faced was the fact that Kansas City was mainly a distribution center with few major corporations. I was fortunate in parlaying my consultation with the Fairbanks Morse Pump Company into a corporate assignment with

Colt Industries, but most of my local clients were small independent businesses.

Two of the larger corporations in Kansas City, Hallmark Cards and the Business Men's Assurance Company of America (BMA), were successful companies and wonderful corporate citizens. I came to recognize that if a capable, well-educated college graduate wanted to locate permanently in the Kansas City area, either Hallmark or BMA would be a first choice. My associate, Harvey Thomas, was the consulting psychologist at Hallmark. That left BMA for me.

BMA was chartered by the state of Missouri in 1909 through the creative efforts of an entrepreneurial salesman by the name of W. T. (Tom) Grant. The company experienced ups and downs selling accident insurance policies, but Grant was nimble in developing sales strategies, and the company built a reputation as a reliable company that met its obligations. The operation of the company was managed by J. C. Higdon, who was generally acknowledged as being an outstanding manager.

By the start of World War II, the company had evolved into a multidimensional, successful company selling a large variety of health, life, and accident insurance policies through a nationwide network of sales offices and agents. Among the sales accomplishments was the establishment of multiple product sales to members of associated groups.

After the war, the company seized on the opportunity to reinsure policies of other companies, becoming a national leader in the reinsurance field, with a talented group of representatives covering the country. With its outstanding national sales and reinsurance organizations,

BMA established monopolistic relationships with its clients, ensuring a steady flow of substantial revenue.

Tom Grant died in 1954, and J. C. Higdon continued his company management with the new title of president. Tom Grant's son, W. D. (Bill), was a graduate of the University of Kansas and earned an MBA at the Wharton School of Finance at the University of Pennsylvania.

Grant took on a generalist role in management as chairman, including the building of the BMA Tower home office of twenty stories, considered to be an architectural masterpiece, furnished with Native American artifacts and western paintings by renowned artists such as Peter Hurd and Frederic James. The American Institute of Architecture gave the BMA Tower its award for outstanding high-rise construction in 1963. Both the building and its interior became so famous that they were included in many art books used by international students learning the elements of architecture and interior design.

Several years prior to my working with BMA, I interviewed an architect who had been involved with the construction of a twenty-story office building in downtown Kansas City. He had remarked that the twenty-story BMA building was built in the same year but at double the cost of the downtown office building. I knew that BMA was a substantial company.

My introduction to BMA came from a speech I gave at a monthly luncheon for human resource directors attended by Bob Le Bow, the HR director at BMA. Le Bow took me under his wing, first promoting me, wearing down resistance until I was given an opportunity to sell myself to a BMA management group, and then he took the lead in scheduling my consulting visits. I spent over twenty years on a routine schedule working with BMA until the company was sold in 1990.

As with all new clients, I assessed and provided feedback to the president and CEO, Bill Grant, and then systematically had sessions with the senior vice presidents, all of whom had been in their positions for at least several years and all of whom had excellent backgrounds of experience and knowledge about the company and their specific functions.

As I completed my assessments, I realized what it was like consulting in a large successful traditional company in which senior management had already achieved their career goals and were preparing for their retirements by developing the people under them. I found immediate acceptance from the senior staff, looking for assistance in selecting and guiding their subordinates, but also from the subordinate staff, welcoming the opportunity to meet with the psychologist who might help them reach their career goals.

It was enlightening and gratifying to find that I was recognized as the "BMA psychologist" and quickly integrated into the system. I represented a new responsibility accorded to Bob Le Bow and HR who now scheduled my time and administered my tests. The message in the company was clear: "If you want to get ahead, you need to see the psychologist." With positive reports from the early assessment candidates, there was an eagerness "to get on the list." Each of my consulting visits also provided unlimited time to executives to discuss individual issues.

BMA became an important part of my life. Not only did it provide a predictable source of activity and income, but it also was a source of community recognition and lifelong friendships. Kansas City at that time had a unique population distribution in which a large percentage of business executives and professional practitioners all gravitated to a few clustered suburban cities in Johnson County, Kansas. Residents tended to join the same clubs and children to attend the same schools.

BMA was typical of the traditional large American company that emerged after World War II. They had established life and health insurance products and an established sales structure, creating a quasi-monopolistic enterprise. They hired outstanding candidates looking for career positions. They were structured with layers of management, so that each recruit could see a path to the top as the preceding group moved up. J. C. Higdon was a competent, organized, involved president guiding the company in its growth.

W. D. (Bill) Grant as President/CEO

With the retirement of J. C. Higdon, Bill Grant took on the role of president in addition to being CEO. Bill Grant was a generalist with diverse interests, such as overseeing the construction of the BMA Tower, starting an insurance company in Australia, and acquiring real estate ventures, television stations, and venture capital acquisitions. It was reported that Grant's diversification strategies accounted for a nearly 40 percent contribution to the company's profitability in 1969. Grant demonstrated his entrepreneurial talents by diversifying earnings from the insurance holdings.

My involvement was only with BMA insurance. With his diverse interests, Grant delegated the operation of the company to two senior vice presidents, each with distinct areas of accountability and each with a high degree of autonomy. The first area, under the senior vice president of sales, included the line functions of insurance sales, reinsurance, and investments. The second staff area, under the senior vice president of administration, included practically everything else, including all administrative, operations, financial, claims, and technical areas.

Sales functions, under J. Kenneth (Kenny) Higdon, the son of J. C. Higdon, were outstanding. Kenny Higdon earned a bachelor's degree in business from the University of Kansas in 1948. He worked with BMA from 1956 to 1987, moving through sales and serving as president from 1977 to 1987. Serving as senior vice president of sales, he had a group of eight bright, enthusiastic regional vice presidents, each responsible for the BMA sales offices in their regions. Reinsurance had a group of four regional vice presidents responsible for calling on smaller life insurance companies in their designated regions.

Both functions had excellent, self-sufficient people operating with clear mission statements, accountabilities, and progress reports. In addition to income raised through investment, they provided significant financing for the corporation.

The senior vice president of administration was also a highly capable person. I remember him as an active, intense, outgoing person totally involved and aware of everything going on around him. He was a protégé of J. C. Higdon, with special status in the organization. He also reminded me of my top sergeant in the Air Force. He was tough and demanding but always protective of his people.

For most of my tenure with BMA, I worked closely with Kenny Higdon in both of his roles. The role of a regional sales vice president was one of considerable authority, managing multiple sales offices in the region, a responsibility that generated a sizable amount of the company income. Each region also had unique challenges. For example, the state of Wisconsin was organized with an association created for dairy farmers that provided insurance for most of the dairy farmers in the state. Disruptions in the dairy market, which did occur, had a significant impact on earnings.

Regional vice presidents were on the road most of the time. Kenny Higdon held regular staff meetings when they were in town. The meetings were interactive discussions of issues, plans, and strategies. I occasionally sat in on the meetings and found them to resemble group dynamics meetings by their degree of open communication. A proportion of my consulting time was always available to anyone in the group on an as-needed basis.

Most regional vice presidents were happy with their jobs, but as a group they were ambitious about their careers. Kenny Higdon and Bill Sayler both advanced from senior vice president of sales to president of the company. Ken Louis was hired directly from his regional position to become president and subsequently chairman of the board of the Ameritas Life Insurance Company. The largest group to leave either became individual producers or managers of BMA sales offices, all with a substantial raise in income.

BMA was a typical post–World War II firm with a top-down organizational structure in a field soon to be dominated by technology-driven companies. BMA was a desirable place to work, and family connections were commonplace. It was a benevolent company that was hesitant to eliminate positions. BMA had a reputation as a leading community-minded company. The senior vice president of administration used his authority to retain BMA's fine reputation.

Unlike my close relationship with the sales and reinsurance groups, I did not spend as much time in operations and administration areas.

The senior vice president prided himself on his own competence in overseeing his well-qualified groups.

The technology impact on large insurance companies was sporadic but inexorable. Large companies with high overheads found their markets systematically eroding as smaller enterprises could use technology to attack individual segments of the market. For example, a plethora of storefront companies captured the term insurance market from major insurers by selling products online at a fraction of the price a large company needed merely to break even.

As early as the 1960s, insurance companies recognized that the IT function would need to undergo massive changes in evolving from manual- to technology-driven systems. BMA had an outstanding IT group with a core of experienced programmers. Most insurance companies looked to outside software vendors to provide the integrated software systems for the future. BMA wrote its own software with its own employees.

J. Kenneth (Kenny) Higdon as President

In 1977, W. T. (Tom) Grant, Bill Grant's son, shared, then later assumed, the role of CEO. Kenny Higdon was promoted to president, and William J. (Bill) Sayler was promoted to senior vice president of sales. With the autonomy Bill Grant had delegated in the past, Higdon's actual authority over administration and operations was limited. He initiated a long-term campaign, focusing primarily on increasing earnings and improving efficiency in operations as opportunities arose.

The company strategy at that time was to keep health insurance affordable for employers and employees alike. The early 1980s were a time of record inflation and skyrocketing interest rates, reducing the sales of traditional life insurance policies, and increased claims of individual health insurance plans. This was a period of creative challenge in which BMA developed new policies such as interest-sensitive contracts.

Higdon was an analytical person who understood the markets and made timely marketing decisions, but he also understood the meld of the operating parts and the difficulty maintaining profitability. We met routinely, with me sharing my informal action research results and observations of the company.

William J. (Bill) Sayler as President

Higdon retired in 1987, and Bill Sayler took over as president. Sayler's career was totally committed to BMA. He, like Higdon, was the son of a senior BMA executive. In addition to broad sales and management experience, Sayler had a natural social warmth and sincerity that projected him into leadership positions with most groups.

These were changing, struggling times in the industry, and the company was moving away from medical and hospital insurance into mainstream life and annuity programs. Sayler had the task of maintaining an existing presence in declining markets, while also creating an infrastructure in new markets.

The contribution to earnings derived from Bill Grant's investments helped cushion the loss in insurance sales. Although I was not involved typically with noninsurance companies, I was involved with two profitable investments initiated by the Grants.

Tenenbaum-Hill

Bill Grant was traveling by air in a first-class seat next to Wayne Tenenbaum, a lawyer by training and a partner in the firm of Tenenbaum-Hill (T-H), a national tax reappraisal firm. The owners were Tenenbaum, a technical genius, and Ken Hill, a superstar salesman who had spent his career in the reappraisal field. In addition to national business, T-H was starting a new project based on a recent Missouri state reappraisal of commercial property that was to last at least four years.

By the time the plane landed, Grant decided he wanted to buy the company. I assessed the partners and key employees and provided excellent reports on all participants. I was working with BMA and took on T-H as a client also. After Ken Hill's untimely death, J. W. Jones, Bob Le Bow's replacement as HR director, assumed Ken's role at T-H. I first worked with J. W. in his role as HR director at Puritan-Bennett.

Hill had developed an outstanding sales organization comprised of men and women with histories as workers in political campaigns. They had multiple contacts throughout the state. Tenenbaum oversaw the technicians who prepared the pleas. The business model was ideal. The client's only payment came from a successful lower reappraisal, and they only pursued clients with a high probability of reappraisal success.

Lab One

The second company, turned up by Tom Grant, was Lab One, a company that did lab tests for insurance companies on insureds with prior medical restrictions. The owner of Lab One was an entrepreneurial chemist who set up labs for different purposes, hired and trained people to perform different tasks, and then sold the companies.

Grant had me assess the people in the company. My conclusion was that no one in the company could run it; Tom would have to hire someone to run the company. I personally didn't think it was such a good investment. A short time after BMA and a group of BMA executives, headed by the Grants, bought the company, an announcement was made that a test for AIDS would be required of anyone purchasing life insurance in the future. Business, of course, boomed and the company was taken public at a great profit.

With declining profits and the prospect of a large impending investment in new software technology, the board of directors in late 1989 sought a buyer for the company's insurance operations. In 1990, the company's insurance operations were acquired by Assicurazioni Generali, an international insurance holding company.

Approximately a year prior to the announcement of the sale, BMA had a major reduction in staff. The financial crisis at BMA seemed to catch most employees by surprise. For a company that rarely eliminated positions, a reduction of nonessential positions was a shock. My involvement with the company was mostly eliminated. I did not continue working with Generali after the sale.

Under Generali, the company reduced overhead even more dramatically and shifted markets into fixed rate annuities, financial services, life reinsurance, and nonmedical insurance products. Generali purchased Jones & Babson, a no-load funds firm based in Kansas City, that managed approximately $2 billion worth of investors' money. In 1994, BMA sold its group and individual medical insurance business in order to focus fully on financial services, life reinsurance, and nonmedical insurance products.

The purchase of the company by the Generali Group had stabilized BMA's financial position and allowed BMA management to concentrate on increasing its margin of profitability.

Walter W. Ross, Walter W. Ross & Company, Inc.

Beta Sigma Phi is a nonacademic sorority with 200,000 members in chapters around the world. Founded in Abilene, Kansas, in 1931 by Walter W. Ross, the organization spread to every state of the United States, to every Canadian province, and to thirty other countries. The sorority was founded for the social, cultural, and civic enrichment of its members. Through various programs, each member is encouraged to grow personally, while at the same time participating in the growth of sisters.

Walter W. (Bill) Ross III was the son of Walter W. Ross Jr. and Doro-thy Eagle Ross and was born in Kansas City in 1923. He was a Navy World War II veteran and a graduate of Westminster College in Fulton, Missouri. In 1945, he joined the company founded by his father and became chief executive officer in 1953. He spent sixty-five years with the company.

His brother, John J. (Jack) Ross Sr., was born in 1927 and also a grad-uate of Westminster College, joined the company in 1947 and spent sixty-three years with the company, primarily as chief operating officer. Bill died in 2009 and Jack died in 2010.

I consulted with the company from approximately 1967 to 1974. I interviewed and had regular meetings with key staff workers, but I worked most closely with Bill and Jack Ross. One of the highlights of my early contacts was spending an afternoon with Walter W. Ross, Bill and Jack's father, the creator of Walter W. Ross & Company, Inc.'s "product," Beta Sigma Phi International.

His story struck me as amazing when I first heard and read about him. A story of how a man in the depth of the Depression created an organization bringing meaning and fullness in the lives of generations of young women, while also creating a respectable living and career for himself and generations of his family to follow, was nothing short of inspirational.

Walter Ross told me about a popular saying during the Depression. Whenever a man had reached his limit of steady unemployment and decided to move on to a new town, one of his relatives would plead, "If you get work, write!" By 1931, Walter Ross had figured out a way to take his job with him. He traveled through Kansas, Missouri, and Oklahoma selling books. Although the country was in a depression, there were still small businesses providing the necessities of life, and surprisingly, most businesses employed young women in store sales, clerical, or "girl Friday" roles.

Women bought books. His task was to get them to buy more books, and his plan was to form chapters of book clubs through "The National 'What to Read' Club." Walter Ross learned from his experiences. From research sources, I learned that Vinita, Oklahoma, played a critical role in his life. Leona Schroers was the city librarian, and she agreed to help with the establishment of a chapter in Vinita. She also introduced Walter Ross to Sally Rogers McSpadden, sister of the famous humorist Will Rogers. McSpadden was a community leader, active in the Oklahoma Federation of Women's Clubs, in addition to other women's volunteer organizations.

McSpadden soon convinced Walter Ross that the organization should be changed from an association to its present form and that the name must really be changed. With her suggestions and Schroers's assistance, a new framework for the organization was developed, and the Greek letter name grew out of the motto chosen for the nonacademic sorority.

The letters beta, sigma, and phi were the first letters of the Greek words for life, learning, and friendship.[12]

In 1932, Beta Sigma Phi was incorporated under a charter granted by the state of Missouri. Walter W. Ross & Company, Inc. owned Beta Sigma Phi. A fee was required to join, and an annual membership fee to be paid by each member provided immediate working capital and a clear focus on a goal of increasing chapters. Membership provided a sorority pin, direct communications from and with the international staff, and a copy of *The Torch*, a monthly newsletter.

Beta Sigma Phi primarily was a social and cultural organization that incorporated service as part of its activities. In addition to the international constitution and bylaws, each chapter composed its own set of bylaws. The intention was to encourage each chapter to expand its own activities within the parameters set by the international organization. This strategy, although a key element in the development of chapters, was also a problem to be addressed when a chapter breached the parameters set by the international organization.

Walter's two sons, Bill and Jack, spent their careers in the business, as defined by Walter Ross, as "outside" and "inside." Bill Ross as president headed the marketing effort and maintained close communication with chapters, including time spent on the road at state conventions and representing the company at special chapter events. Jack Ross was responsible for all administrative functions.

The evolution of Beta Sigma Phi was a continuous challenge for Bill Ross and Jack Ross and the international staff headquartered in Kansas City. Beta Sigma Phi was committed to providing continuous service, in enhancing the commitment and effectiveness of chapters, and in the marketing challenge of adding new chapters. Unlike academic sororities, Beta Sigma Phi was a commercial enterprise that required constant monitoring of its business plan.

Through the years, small and sometimes large problems forced some changes or enhancements in operating procedures. Initially, the organization grew through the efforts of a field staff setting up new chapters in specific territories. Members were also encouraged to assist in helping new chapter development. Once a critical mass of chapters was attained, a management reorganization in the structure and mission of each chapter had a profound effect on future growth and profitability. The reorganization dictated that when a chapter increased its members by a designated number, it was required to assist in the colonization of new, independent chapters.

The marketing function had always been responsive to chapter needs and accomplishments. The state convention was a powerful tool. By assisting in the coordination and with Bill Ross attending each state convention, a mutual trust and bonding was developed with chapter officers. Division chairmen were always available for members to contact. The Walter W. Ross staff were housed in an impressive office building in south Kansas City that members were encouraged to visit.

When I consulted with the company fifty years ago, time was spent on each visit brainstorming with Bill Ross, Jack Ross, and the marketing staff discussing issues that had arisen and strategies and programs that could be initiated. I was always impressed by how everyone seemed to be aware of what was going on in the chapters.

A continuous issue involved chapters gravitating away from the parameters set by the company. The strongest members would become leaders, and some power struggles were inevitable; those issues would be addressed immediately. The number one issue involved maintaining the authority of Walter W. Ross & Company.

In perusing information about Beta Sigma Phi that is available today, I noticed a statement that "today Beta Sigma Phi is a non-profit corporation," followed by, "which maintains a contract with Walter W. Ross & Company for complete business management of all of its affairs."

Communication between the home office and the chapters was always a high priority. The IT function was on the cutting edge of available technology, a trend that has continued through the years.

In the material Beta Sigma Phi sends to prospective members, the mission statement has not changed, but the Internet has enhanced communication dramatically. Aside from immediate contact with all division chairmen and all departments, more than fifty downloads address everything from financial/administrative considerations to audio and video links, party plan ideas, and special offers for members.

The Torch has grown from its inception as a four-page bulletin into a magazine of thirty-two pages. In addition to providing information and a link between active members, it also publishes stories and poems by members, runs personality sketches of its honorary members and others, and runs contests for short stories and poetry.

Its many notable and honorary members included Sara Ophelia Cannon (a. k. a.) Minnie Pearl, Eleanor Roosevelt, Pat Nixon, Barbara Bush, Hillary Clinton, Elizabeth Dole, Anne Fisher, Rosalynn Carter, Louise Faulkner, Joan Fontaine, Debbie Reynolds, Olympia Snowe, Senator Muriel Humphrey, Eunice Kennedy Shriver, Ruth Warrick, Lillian Carter, Mrs. Barry Goldwater, Agnes Moorehead, Ginger Rogers, Grandma Moses, Rosalind Russell, Sue Scott, Margaret Chase Smith, Mrs. Spencer Tracy, Vera Ford, and Earlene Fowler.

The following is an update of Beta Sigma Phi today:

> Typical chapters enjoy socials that range from informal gatherings to gala affairs that often include friends and family. Fascinating cultural programs offer insight into subjects that range from arts to gardening to in-home businesses. Membership in our organization provides opportunities to contribute to your community, develop lifelong friendships, and polish leadership skills.

> Our members raise more than $3 million for local charities and donate over 200,000 volunteer hours in an average year. Each chapter determines its own service projects and participation is always voluntary. Chapters have created their own International Funds that donate millions of dollars to health research groups, hunger projects, and other worthwhile causes.

> Members and their families can receive assistance through our International Loan Scholarship and Disaster Funds. What makes us unique? Unlike a college sorority, our organization has members of all ages and educational backgrounds. Our sisterhood constantly redefines itself through the diversity and vitality of its members who share their ideas, talents, and enthusiasm.

> This is why we are known around the world as "The Friendship Organization."

In any management course, studying the entrepreneurial genius of Walter W. Ross should hold a high priority. In his due diligence, he was able to shift his model from the concrete task of selling books to the conceptual model of opening a new world of personal expansion for women who both pay for and work toward recruiting new prospects. Fees (not dues) are collected annually in advance to pay for services, administration, and sales. A structure was established whereby chapters did their own recruiting. When a chapter reached a designated limit, it was responsible for starting a new chapter.

After eighty-seven years, the model established by Walter W. Ross not only is valid but also continues to serve and to show significant growth.

James H. (Jim) Barickman, Barickman Advertising

James H. Barickman was born in 1924 in Minneapolis, Minnesota. He was a veteran of World War II. After the war, he received a BS in business and finance from the University of Minnesota. He began his career in the marketing department of the Pillsbury Company and later moved to Kansas City, Missouri, to begin his advertising career with Bruce B. Brewer Company. His strategy was to become involved in civic leadership as the president of the Junior Chamber of Commerce and Junior Achievement. He also served as city councilman in Fairway, Kansas, and was chairman of the Johnson County Nixon-Lodge presidential campaign in 1960.

One of my favorite movies of all time is *The Man in the Gray Flannel Suit*, with Gregory Peck, from a book by Sloan Wilson about the wild 1950s and 1960s in the New York advertising and public relations world and the life of the top-dog rainmakers. An even wilder takeoff on Sloan Wilson's work is the *Mad Men* TV series.

In 1959, with only two employees, Jim Barickman opened the Kansas City office of the Winius-Brandon Company, a creative St. Louis advertising agency known for innovative advertising campaigns such as "Speedy Alka-Seltzer." Along with Winius-Brandon's creativity, he added his own creative and technical staffs. His special concentration was building a professional staff of talented account executives capable of developing strong personal and professional relationships with clients. Jim's reputation grew with the company, and he personally controlled numerous hip-pocket accounts. In 1967, with an investment from an outside financial firm, he started his own company in Kansas City— Barickman Advertising.

In the lexicon of the advertising industry, the term *hip-pocket account* describes an account that is owned by the agent servicing the account, rather than the agency that controls the account. The agent with a hip-pocket account can command a high salary, but if the agent decides to leave the agency, the account leaves with the agent.

There are three ways to earn a hip-pocket account:

1. By being extremely creative in handling the account
2. By being close friends with the president of the account company
3. By having accomplished both one and two

Jim Barickman and Don Draper, the rainmaker in *Mad Men*, had both the creativity and the contact with the deciding person in their hip-pocket accounts. When Jim Barickman started his own company, he brought in captive accounts and was off and running. Unlike Don Draper, who experienced ambivalence before deciding to head for the top, Jim Barickman knew where he was heading from the start.

From my consulting relationship with Rick Harman at Myron Green Cafeterias, I was referred to Jim Barickman. At the time, I didn't know Barickman, but we were both friends of Harman and all three of us were members of the Beta Theta Pi fraternity. In a meeting in Barickman's office, I explained what I did, hoping to sell my services. It turned out that Harman had already sold me, and Barickman simply wanted to set up a schedule. By the time I started consulting with Barickman Advertising in 1970, they were already the largest advertising agency between the Mississippi River and the West Coast.

My first interviews were with Barickman and his two key managers, his manager of account executives and his manager of technical/creative services. I systematically assessed all managers and account executives, quickly becoming integrated into a broad consulting role.

Jim Barickman was a highly intelligent, analytical person who zeroed in quickly on where he was heading. He was a man's man. He was a high-stakes gin rummy player who won more than he lost. He was a fun guy who liked to drink and was quick to pick up the check. He had a legitimate fifteen golf handicap and could be counted on to come through under pressure.

Advertising is a tight, competitive industry. The top people are well known and gravitate to the top firms—like Barickman did. An advertising agency is also a complex business with account executives focused on existing and prospective clients, and the technical and creative staff addressing a myriad of high-pressure daily deadlines and detail.

I was impressed with the quality and capability of the people I assessed and with their interest and enthusiasm in the assessment program. Rather than dealing primarily with Barickman, I had as my main contacts the two key managers overseeing respectively the account executives and the technical/creative staff. Both were keenly interested in the personal development of their staffs, and I always had a full schedule of activity during my consulting visits.

Jim Barickman had a clear overview of his company, but he never forgot his role as rainmaker. He could do more for the company spending an afternoon playing high stakes gin rummy than he could involving himself with company detail. His technical staff were experienced and highly competent. He met daily with his staff and knew what was going on, but he didn't intervene. He had confidence in their capability.

Advertising people tend to be individualistic and sensitive, and an inordinate number of personal crises were inevitable. I loved working with Barickman. Aside from interacting with an interesting, independent staff, I became an important company resource as an authority for dealing with the inevitable crises.

Crises came in all shapes. I intervened in personal quarrels. I made referrals for therapy. My visits were for the whole day, and I spent time just being a sounding board.

One afternoon, Jim saw me at the country club to which we both belonged and asked me to help him with a crisis. He was about to play with a foursome that included the chairman of one of Barickman's largest clients, when the client's partner had to drop out. Jim asked me if I could play and drive the client in my golf cart, which I agreed to do. Jim didn't tell me that the client was too intoxicated to drive the cart himself, which led to another crisis. After a few holes, Jim admonished me for not parking in the shade. The client was about to pass out!

I also learned a lot about business in general. With its diverse base of clients, Barickman always had daily issues with clients, reasonable or unreasonable, which required management strategies for some clients and priority setting for others. I was always impressed with how managers collaboratively seemed to resolve the day-to-day issues.

Although Jim Barickman was competitive, he was uncomfortable dealing with personnel issues. He had difficulty saying "no" to people. To compensate, he hired a surrogate president to handle administrative detail. He was a menacing, no-nonsense person whose favorite word was "no." By having his surrogate start with a "no," Jim had time to consider his decisions carefully. Even playing gin rummy, Jim knew that his company was in good hands.

The lifeblood of the company were the account executives who saw their jobs as never-ending but also with the potential to be highly rewarding. A story I heard involved the experience of Al Coleman, the account manager for the Rival Manufacturing Company in Kansas City. Steve Talge, the president of Rival, told Coleman that he needed a name for a slow-cooking pot by the next day. That night, he was watching a TV special on campus turmoil in which the troublemakers were referred to as crackpots, and the word stuck. At 1:30 a.m., Coleman jumped out of bed and scribbled "crock pot" on a sheet of paper, and a million-dollar brand name was born.

Mad Men is an extreme takeoff on the advertising business during the era of my involvement with Barickman Advertising. In the TV series, everyone always has a lit cigarette; extramarital affairs are the rule, not the exception; executives have open bars in their offices; and all account executives are devious. I found the Barickman account executives to be intelligent, enthusiastic, and industrious, but they also were professional salespeople with some of the normal idiosyncrasies expected in an outgoing personality. They also had a special lexicon. Success was measured in terms of hitting "big casino!"

As the company grew, an office was opened in Denver. For an advertising agency without a direct New York connection, Barickman had an impressive list of national accounts, including Western Auto, Green Giant, Pillsbury, Hallmark Cards, Lee (the maker of jeans), the Safeway chain, and Rival Manufacturing. It was rated the forty-second largest advertising agency in the United States; it did business worldwide.

In 1980, Barickman Advertising was acquired by Doyle Dane Bernbach, at that time, the eighth-largest advertising company in the world. Barickman was a senior vice president of Doyle Dane Bernbach and later chairman of the board of Barkley Evergreen & Partners in Kansas City.

Barickman died in 2008 at the age of eighty-one. He was a classic example of the great American successful entrepreneur who through his own intelligence, talent, drive, and risk tolerance achieves amazing success. From the start, he had a mission. He created his network of friends and contacts. He cultivated his own hip-pocket accounts that were the foundation of his enterprise. He created an enterprise that built on his strengths and compensated for his weaknesses. When he sold his enterprise, it was at a peak value.

Forrest T. Jones, Forrest T. Jones & Company

Forrest T. Jones is a perfect example of a man pulling himself up with industriousness, guile, and personal development. Starting with Allstate in Chicago in the 1940s selling insurance supplies on commission to independent agents, he came up with a plan whereby he personally would deliver, stock, and reorder supplies for customers—relieving them of these tasks while locking in a growing client base. With additional business, he added clerical staff under his wife, Dottie, as he expanded sales, furthering growth.

He also recognized a need to make his image more professional so that he could operate on the same playing field as his customers. With the help of Dottie, he worked on his diction, neutralizing a rural twang and adding a repertoire of expressions appropriate for social encounters. He became a voyeur of sorts, quietly studying social mannerisms of successful people and adopting a casual style of relating to others.

In 1953, the Joneses seized an opportunity to purchase a small insurance agency in Kansas City that sold insurance and financial products to associations. The company has since grown to 250 employees, managed by their son Richard, selling group health and life products primarily to school systems and associations.

I was introduced to Forrest Jones through one of my clients, Bill Ross, president of Walter W. Ross & Company, the company servicing over 200,000 female members affiliated with its nonacademic sorority, Beta Sigma Phi. Jones explained that Ross was so positive about my work with Beta Sigma Phi, that he wanted me to work with him at Forrest T. Jones. We set a date for me to assess both Forrest and Dottie Jones.

The assessment with Forrest Jones went well. He was obviously an extremely capable person, and I was impressed with his drive and resourcefulness. He handled the interview well, elaborating on his own self-assessment and the steps he had taken for self-improvement.

When I completed my interview, I realized that Forrest Jones now had his own agenda. In a well-organized presentation, he explained the services that Forrest T. Jones (FTJ) provided and what a great service and financial coup Beta Sigma Phi would enjoy by signing up with FTJ. He further explained what a great friend I would be to Ross by encouraging him to sign up.

At first, I was surprised, but then I realized I was seeing what made Jones so successful. Beta Sigma Phi was a target that warranted a full-court press, and Jones was not about to let any opportunity pass. I was not about to take the bait Jones was offering, and I knew that Beta Sigma Phi never tried to sell things to their members.

I also was impressed by my interview with Dottie Jones. She lacked her husband's conceptual skills and creativity, but she was totally focused on her goals. She had a business college education, and she was the administrative, detail-minded person in the company who saw that systems were in place and that everyone knew what they were expected to do. She was a working manager, with a set of four-by-six cards for her tasks of the day. She tended to view things in black or white and worked best dealing with tangible issues.

It was a great team. Forrest Jones concentrated on establishing personal relationships with designated leaders, primarily school superintendents and association leaders, and Dottie ran the operation. Their roles had not changed appreciably from their days in Chicago, but they were operating at a much higher level.

Although Bill Ross did not sign up with FTJ, Forrest and Dottie Jones continued to follow through on the program whereby I provided assessment and feedback sessions with their key employees. The company was not large enough to support an ongoing relationship, but I maintained a long-term relationship in interviewing new or rising people in the organization and assisting in ad hoc issues.

The company continued to grow, both in size and profitability. They added new employees both in operations and sales, bought a 20,000-square-foot office building, and installed state-of-the art computer systems.

There was a critical incident in my dealing with Forrest and Dottie Jones that was regrettable but understandable. A key executive from a client company in Kansas City accepted a senior executive position in Des Moines with the General United Insurance Company, a newly formed enterprise that merged five smaller insurance companies. With his management background in a large company, the executive's contributions to the organization were outstanding, but his family was unhappy in Des Moines. He asked if I was familiar with any opportunities in Kansas City. When I mentioned his availability to Forrest Jones, he jumped at the opportunity to hire the available executive.

Unfortunately, after two months the executive was fired. My post-case analysis concluded that the timing was premature and that potential talents of the executive were neither recognized nor seen as needed. It was a classic case of a large company executive with general management skills simply not fitting into a first-generation, entrepreneurial company in which competence is measured by tasks accomplished. It was a scene I came to recognize and see often as large companies had massive reductions in force.

Forrest Jones died in 1994; Dottie Jones died in 2009. When their son, Richard Jones, came into the company's leadership, the need for broader scope management was recognized. I was not involved with the company at the time, but Richard Jones attacked the problem with outside consultants. The company today is much larger with a diversified product line.

FTJ was a company with low overhead and limited employees performing specific tasks. Money was invested in technology to improve product availability and service. It was an ideal basic company that could weather economic downturns and reap the benefits that came with long-term recognition and growth.

Cliff C. Jones, R. B. Jones and Company

At one time, R. B. Jones in Kansas City was one of the major brokers of commercial insurance in the country and an example of an old-money company. Started in the 1880s by R. B. Jones, it served as a platform for the education and employment of his sons and grandsons. The company has not existed for years, and its former chairman, Cliff C. Jones Jr., who retired in 1975, died in 2014 at the age of ninety-four.

The Jones families were prominent in civic and social circles in Kansas City and were members of the tightly knit Kansas City Country Club, in which members were selected by local heritage. The country club was considered by its members to be so exclusive that it was referred to simply as the "Club."

The ultimate sale of a commercial insurance policy requires a prospective buyer, a salesperson to present and finalize the sale, and a servicer to handle the processing and administration. R. B. Jones had a perfect three-tier system. For example, Cliff Jones would contact a business owner friend at the Club, inquiring about sending an agent to see him (first tier), the salesman would finalize the transaction (second tier), and the lowest-paid tier member, the servicer, would handle the work.

The system worked perfectly. Jones's sales numbers were astronomical. The only problem was that the Club was so exclusive, significant growth was limited. The solution was to entice independent agents to become associates by moving into the R. B. Jones building and renting office space and servicer support. The company was able to bring in some outstanding producers with loyal, hip-pocket national accounts.

I had a friend, Lloyd Lynd, who was both a successful commercial broker associated with R. B. Jones and an entrepreneur with other business interests. Lynd hired me to assess various individuals who either worked for him or were candidates for employment. He also urged the president of R. B. Jones to consider using my services.

John Tucker, the president (not a family member), was highly competent. He controlled all facets of the company, and he was quick to identify and resolve issues. He had a plan for growth that included hiring experienced brokers but also buying the business of associated partners and turning them into employees. He saw an immediate need for me, and suddenly I had a prestige Kansas City client with an outstanding national reputation. I consulted with R. B. Jones for approximately ten years, systematically assessing key staff in both the Kansas City and the New York City offices and providing project and research assignments for specific executives.

Most brokers were highly competent with technical, sales, and management skills. Most had extensive contacts in business and with insurance underwriters. They in effect ran complicated, profitable, entrepreneurial businesses but used R. B. Jones for professional identification and technical support.

A major project involved assisting in the preparation for a public offering, requiring departmental reorganizations and personnel reallocations, including the elimination of some functions and people. I thought the R. B. Jones management handled the personnel eliminations in a reasonably compassionate manner.

With the public offering, most employees were to get a minimum bonus of at least $25,000 ($100,000 in today's dollars). A moratorium on firing was put in place three months before the offering, although the individuals to be replaced were already known. The managers also agreed on generous separation settlements. I was aware of an employee, scheduled to be terminated, whose tenure fell within the three-month moratorium period. After receiving his bonus, he resigned from the company and invested his bonus in a McDonald's franchise, from which he became quite successful.

The public offering was the apotheosis, preceding a steady decline and ultimately a merging with another organization. The R. B. Jones ties with their independent brokers were related mostly to the monetary advantage available to the brokers through the R. B. Jones relationship. They had hip-pocket control over their clients. Although noncompete agreements were commonplace in the industry, exercising them was difficult and expensive. Key agents were systematically picked off by a new rival organization. My tenure with the company ended during the period of the decline.

Although the company had lost its edge, it was still a major broker in the field. It was involved subsequently in multiple mergers.

This memoir is about executives with whom I have consulted. Although he was not strategically involved in day-to-day management,

Cliff Jones was an outstanding person whose presence in the company afforded instant credibility. He graduated cum laude from Princeton University in 1941 with a degree in economics and served as a combat naval officer during World War II. Although he had positions as president, CEO, and chairman of the board, he was known for his philanthropy and personal involvement in civic and community activities, such as president/chairman of the Greater Kansas City Chamber of Commerce.

Jones took an early retirement from the company in 1975 at the age of 55, entering the Department of Religious Studies at the University of Kansas in a three-year master's degree program. He maintained partial ownership in several financial enterprises and served on at least ten corporate boards. His obituary lists almost a page of civic, religious, and philanthropic organizations in which he was actively involved.

Most of my involvement in the company was through the president, but Jones and I formed a personal relationship. With his philosophy and religious interests, he found common ground with a psychologist. He became involved with motivational speaking and wrote a book on business ethics. We spent many lunches together discussing his activities and ideas.

For a person active in a competitive business, he always found time to share in the problems of others and to help them directly. He had a cousin in the company with a gambling problem who forfeited the inherited company stock he used as collateral. Jones paid his debt, regained his stock, and had me meet periodically with him. A granddaughter's husband was having a career crisis and Jones had me counsel him.

Jones spent the later days of his life in continuous care and assisted living. As his health deteriorated, he systematically called each of a special group of friends, including me, to schedule an individual lunch with him. This was obviously an ambitious project, but it was typical of his sincerity.

William (Bill) Merrick, Arthur Young & Company

All accounting services for Vulcan Insurance Company in Birmingham, Alabama, were provided by the big eight accounting firm of Arthur Young & Company (AY), one of the top professional service firms in the world. The managing partner, William (Bill) Merrick, worked closely with Dave Noble, considered by Noble as a close friend as well as adviser. John Cooper headed the audit staff serving Vulcan while the tax partner, Joseph (Joe) Nicholls, headed the tax staff. Manager Patrick (Pat) Willingham headed management services projects.

The Birmingham office was recognized as one of AY's top offices. The firm's reputation was so well regarded by the accounting faculty at the University of Alabama that each year the firm usually added to its staff the top three graduates of the university accounting program.

Dave Noble described my contribution to Vulcan Insurance and recommended me to Bill Merrick. After completing my assessment and feedback with Bill Merrick, he agreed to my initiating a program in which I would provide assessment, feedback, and consultation to the AY professional staff. It was a personally rewarding multiyear engagement with some of the brightest and most professional individuals with whom I have ever been associated. As AY staff moved on to new positions, I had limited engagements with offices in Atlanta, New Orleans, and Knoxville, Tennessee, as well as a thirty-plus year relationship with the Drummond Company, Inc., the largest private international coal company in America.

Bill Merrick was a six-foot-tall, hyperactive, intense, outgoing person who was totally involved and aware of everything going on around him. On a new staff person's first day on the job, Merrick began to form a close personal relationship that was reinforced continually. Whenever I met with or interviewed one of his staff, I was buttonholed by Merrick immediately after a session to learn what I thought of the person.

Merrick was demanding but committed totally to helping each of his staff to excel. Like a coach, always aware and involved, Merrick created an esprit de corps. They were top professionals and knew it! With his personal interest in the lives of his staff, he also was supportive when staff members had opportunities for advancement beyond the Birmingham office.

Merrick obviously felt accountable. With everyone, including me, Merrick was quick to point out potential problem issues and to offer friendly advice or observations. At AY, all staff always wore suits with ties to work. Sport coats were not acceptable. Although my other clients did not have dress codes, I intuitively knew that it would bother Bill if I dressed differently than what was standard for an AY consultant.

I spent many years traveling to Alabama each month, often spending time with three different clients. I spent approximately four years consulting with AY, up to the time that Bill Merrick retired. I established many long-term friendships that evolved as AY staff joined the executive groups at Statesman Life, American Life, and the Drummond Company. I first interviewed John Matovina, the present CEO and chairman of American Equity Life, when he was a new staff member of AY, some thirty-five years ago.

After I left Arthur Young, AY merged with Ernst & Company in 1989 to become Ernst & Young (EY), one of the largest professional firms in the world—a big four accounting firm. The big four firms have had an amazing evolution. When I first started consulting with AY, they did not have any female professionals in the company, and they had just hired their first black professional. Females now make up approximately two-thirds of big four professionals.

One of my most interesting AY interviews was with a member of the Birmingham staff who was the first big eight accountant to undertake a management consulting engagement. The individual in question was performing an audit at a local Birmingham hospital. The hospital administrator approached him with a request to undertake a study. The hospital administrator explained that he had a request by the surgeons serving the hospital to add a new surgery unit. He explained that the surgeons played golf on Wednesdays. The surgery unit was not used on Wednesday, but the unit was overcrowded on the other four days. He contracted for a study by AY to determine the effect of scheduling surgeries on Wednesdays.

AY's research showed that a new surgery unit was not needed and a new field of "management services" was born, expanding the service offered by accounting firms to include the full range of management consulting.

Patrick (Pat) Willingham

Pat Willingham was one of the most impressive managers with whom I have worked. Willingham graduated at the top of his class in accounting at the University of Alabama. Starting in auditing with AY, Willingham was perceptive in understanding management structure and in acquiring skills as a management consultant. He headed management services at AY, which included projects for the Drummond Company, Inc., one of the largest private companies in America. He was also interested in the development of his subordinates, and we worked together closely.

Drummond was a small company that had grown dramatically through two major sales efforts, both accomplished by the president of Drummond, Garry N. Drummond. The first was a long-term contract to provide coal to Alabama Power Company at a top-dollar price. A second sale was an exclusive contract to provide coal to Japan. Almost overnight, Drummond had over thirty active surface mines in production throughout the state of Alabama in a company with limited management infrastructure.

Recognizing their deficiencies, Drummond hired key managers from AY, starting with tax partner Joe Nicholls as senior vice president of finance. Pat Willingham joined Nicholls as head of financial operations. Other AY managers and associates were added, including Tom Walters, Tom Hinson, Larry Chamblee, and John Matovina.

With his new position, Willingham contacted me to assist in developing his staff, initiating a consulting relationship with Drummond that lasted over thirty years. Although he made immediate contributions, Willingham recognized that he had limited authority to initiate management direction and change. He decided to leave the company to pursue entrepreneurial opportunities with which he was involved.

The Drummond corporate office was in Birmingham, but the operations center and most employees, including United Mine workers, lived in Jasper, Alabama, approximately sixty miles west of Birmingham in conservative, dry Walker County. When he was with AY, Pat Willingham coordinated a venture in which he and eight physicians active at the Walker County Community Hospital purchased the hospital. Although the hospital had a marginal reputation, it was a financial success due to lucrative health care benefits afforded to United Mine workers. It was a conceded fact that many mine workers added the names of distant relatives to their policies.

The hospital's financial success notwithstanding, it was inefficient, poorly managed, and had marginally qualified staff. Each physician set his own schedule, creating inefficiencies and long waiting periods for patients. In addition to the general inefficiency of the physicians, one of the surgeons was sued by a surgical nurse and declared impaired by the state medical association. Confronted with the reality of his investment, Willingham took on the position of CEO. He selected the most adaptable physician from the group to serve as chief of staff.

By the time I was asked to consult with the hospital, Willingham had made great strides in simply addressing basic issues of organization and planning. My role was to evaluate existing new staff to facilitate group solidarity and to attempt to integrate the physician group into the organizational structure.

My impact working with the staff was successful. A new director of nursing assumed a close working relationship with Pat and his corporate staff, establishing clear operational guidelines, training programs, and interdepartmental communication.

My progress with physicians was not so successful. When I scheduled a group meeting with the physicians to simply open discussion on specific problems and issues, only the chief of staff came to the meeting. Some change and restructuring had taken place at a management level, and Willingham, working with the chief of staff, was able to gain adherence to clear guidelines of acceptable and unacceptable behavior.

I consider my work with the Walker County Hospital as a project rather than an ongoing relationship. Through the years, I lost contact with Pat Willingham, but I kept up with his career. He became the owner/CEO of a company providing medical services and equipment throughout Alabama and Mississippi.

James F. (Jim) O'Crowley Jr., Coalter Investment

Jim O'Crowley had an outstanding career in corporate management, including serving as corporate controller of AT&T during its monopolistic days. He also was a creative entrepreneur who carved a lucrative enterprise out of his management experience.

One day in 1980, I received a call from O'Crowley. He explained that he was the new CEO of a national chain of sporting goods stores headquartered in Kansas City (I can't remember the name). He said that he had always used consulting psychologists. He had gotten my name from someone and we met. He explained the company was failing, and he was hired to see if he could save it. O'Crowley wanted me to evaluate key people to see if I could help him save it.

Ordinarily, I would not accept an assignment that was designed to eliminate jobs. In this case, the staff realized the company was close to bankruptcy and welcomed any contributions I could make.

I spent intense time interviewing existing staff and meeting with O'Crowley. I quickly realized the extent of his business knowledge and competence. He gained confidence from his staff, reorganized job descriptions, and established an action business plan.

His significant actions notwithstanding, within a year, O'Crowley opted to dissolve the company. I came to realize that the company was in worse shape than I had imagined initially and that O'Crowley had made the most realistic decision available for the investors.

When the O'Crowley family moved to Kansas City for his new job, Jim joined a country club of which I was a member, and we became friends. It was after the company was dissolved that I learned how he came to his position in Kansas City and that he was a true entrepreneur with an unusually creative and successful career.

He was a professional CEO. By capitalizing on his broad business knowledge and experience, he designed a marketing niche for someone promoting his exact qualifications. Prior to his assignment in Kansas City, he had filled CEO positions in other troubled companies. He had a one-person company with an established reputation. When he secured a new contract, he brought in various consulting specialists.

As with any enterprise, the sales/marketing strategy is critical. I started my own consulting practice with cold calls and lunch lectures to business groups. Jim developed a descriptive letter directed to the investors in problem companies.

His letter had outstanding success, and it is included verbatim below. The letter defines the facts investors need to know about their investments and the actions required to avoid disastrous results. The wisdom and the professionalism of the letter I consider to be an example to stimulate enthusiasm in an aspiring entrepreneur in any field of endeavor.

COALTER INVESTMENT

In your position, you may be aware of situations where I can be of assistance. It is also possible you know of clients, associates, directors of companies or acquaintances who may have an interest in this letter.

Several years ago, I was approached by a group of institutional lenders seeking examination of a company in which they had made substantial investments. After carefully examining the facts, they asked the following:

1. How long and how much would it cost to determine the viability of the company?
2. If, in my opinion, the company has no future the answer was easy. On the other hand, if I concluded it was viable, how long and how much would it cost to complete a detailed turn-around plan?
3. Having proposed such a plan, would I be willing to assume management responsibility of the firm and implement the plan?

4. As part of this plan, would I seek out and train a new chief executive officer as my replacement?

Coalter Investment was formed by me to do just this. We have a breadth and depth of experience that is rarely matched.

Over the years, I have been amazed at how many companies slip into disastrous conditions before positive action is taken. In most cases, the signals of trouble appear long before the situation becomes terminal. But so often, no one was knowledgeable, willing to admit the existence of trouble, let alone deal with it.

Management often pushes recognition of declining performance into the future hoping to have more time to deal with rapidly deteriorating performance. All too often, recognition of trouble and taking commensurate action is avoided to keep from having the real circumstances known. Boards of directors often lack the time and information to effectively analyze potential disasters. Commercial banks and institutional lenders often deal with incomplete data—data that generally masks the true operating

performance and financial condition of a
company.

When there is evidence of serious
earnings, capital structure and cash
flow problems, time is the most critical
consideration. Properly appraising a
situation and quickly choosing a course
of action may mean the difference between
survival and disaster.

When serious financial trouble develops,
it is almost axiomatic that an objective
internal appraisal is difficult at any
level, if not impossible. This results
from personal and organizational biases
plus pure defensiveness.

There is likely charged emotional "in-
fighting" developing from recriminations
reaching from leaders and the board
to the most senior executives and
beyond. This diversion from operating
the business, assembling the facts and
taking corrective actions results in
a severe loss of time and cash flow.
Seldom do any of the parties involved
understand the magnitude of this loss.
Without the assistance of outside
counsel, not subject to the emotional
and organizational intimidation that

often exists, deterioration of operating performance can drastically accelerate.

To immediately replace senior management is rarely the correct solution. Seldom are the dimensions and requirements known; there is no basis for measuring effectiveness once action is taken; and, more importantly, the qualifications for new executives must be defined relative to an unknown task.

Without a broad plan of action, executives must be analysts, while attempting to operate a business near the brink of disaster. Getting their feet on the ground in a rapidly deteriorating business will cost time and money. This cost can be staggering.

Possibly the largest, most costly personnel mistakes are made by replacing executives without first understanding the requirements of the job. The facts must first be understood to determine these requirements and an orderly plan of action.

Generally speaking, there is seldom a reliable source for individuals having the unique talent to provide counsel to boards, lenders and management

in troubled situations. Never are
these skills learned in large highly
structured, compartmentalized and
successful companies. They are developed
through experience guiding firms through
the trauma of financial disaster, back to
profitability.

This rare type of experience is available
at Coalter Investment. Our capabilities
encompass manufacturing, retailing,
distribution and service-oriented
companies.

I would be pleased to discuss these
capabilities with you.

Sincerely,
James F. O'Crowley Jr.

As a friend, I discovered that O'Crowley loved to talk business, and I spent considerable time taking advantage of his willingness to share his knowledge and experience. He had a facility for breaking complex situations into simple logical propositions.

I remember seeking him out about some investment opportunities I was considering. After a few questions he said, "You want to make money while you sleep. You need an oil well!" He then elaborated on different investments and how each required a specific commitment.

I met with O'Crowley intermittently, and then he left town. I assumed he had another assignment.

Jay Breidenthal, Security National Bank

A prominent Kansas City, Kansas, family tree evolved from the matrimonial joining of Breidenthal and Sutherland families, representing respectively banking and lumbering interests. After graduating from the University of Kansas, Jay Breidenthal worked under his father, who was the president/CEO of the Security National Bank in downtown Kansas City, Kansas. My contact with Breidenthal came in the late 1980s when he was in his late thirties and had assumed the positions of president/CEO of Security National. Through mutual contacts, he knew that I was a psychologist for BMA, and he contacted me.

Security National was a major Kansas Bank with an excellent reputation and strong correspondent banking relationships throughout the state. Though successful, the bank functioned as it had for years in a time when high interest rates stifled new business in a highly competitive market.

Breidenthal was an intelligent, unusually open, unpretentious person, so aware of his inherited financial advantages that he never projected an image other than that of a regular guy. His employees shared information spontaneously, knowing that he was more a trusted comrade than a boss. At the same time, he was only too aware of inefficiencies at the bank that needed to be addressed. From his understanding of my role with BMA, he was interested in Security National developing a similar relationship with me.

Breidenthal and I bonded quickly. We both knew many of the same people, and we both had athletic interests; we were both handball players. There are a limited number of handball courts, mostly in YMCAs, and most people have never heard of the game, much less seen it played. Almost like with bikers, handball is a cult. Handball pushes a person to the ultimate of physical exertion, and players quickly become soul mates.

Breidenthal, being young, had inherited long-term bank employees in key positions of questionable effectiveness. For example, a loan committee of four or five people met twice a week to review loan applications. The loan manager not only would introduce new loans but also would review the information and then informally make a comment regarding whether the loan should be approved. Breidenthal discovered that the committee had never once contradicted the manager's informal comment, causing him to wonder why under that system all those people needed to be on the same committee.

We embarked on an intense schedule in which I assessed both established executives and promising trainees and associates. Breidenthal had done an outstanding job in preparing his staff with individual meetings, informing them that he was going to reorganize and including senior members in the planning.

One of the most constructive activities was a series of organizational development confrontation meetings, leading to a series of organizational changes. Most important symbolically was a revamping of loan application procedures.

My relationship with Breidenthal and the bank staff in general was both rewarding to me and effective in providing management direction. The environment became more oriented to constructive change, with senior staff gravitating into staff assignments or specialty projects and with junior staff assuming broader line authority.

Complexities in the relationships of the bank's owners ultimately led to a sale of the bank in the second year of my consulting relationship with the bank. Jay had part ownership in a small bank in an adjoining county. He took over the presidency and showed a continued pattern of growth. I did not have a consulting arrangement with the new bank.

Before Security National was sold, Breidenthal helped me negotiate a personal loan from Security National that had a profound effect on my professional and financial future. In another chapter, I elaborate on my purchase of Alvarado Manufacturing Company in South El Monte, California. The company was owned by a Kansas City investment group, headed by my personal accountant who controlled the company with 50 percent ownership.

I was contracted to assist in hiring a new president. After completing the assignment, my accountant informed me that several partners wanted to sell their shares and suggested that I might want to buy them. I became a 35 percent stockholder. I subsequently learned that my accountant was in financial difficulty at a time under Fed Chairman Paul Volcker when interest rates were at 20 percent. I also learned that my accountant had sold 5 percent of his holdings, thus no longer had a controlling interest.

I approached Jay Breidenthal for a loan to see if I could buy the company. He said he would cover whatever I needed and negotiate the sale for me. I was so pleased, I offered him a part of the company, which he refused. I then bought out all remaining stockholders and owned 100 percent of the company.

During my time as a Kansas resident, Breidenthal and I remained friends. I continued as an occasional unpaid management adviser to Jay, and he was my unofficial financial adviser.

Dean Lawrence, Unimark

My introduction to Unimark was unique. The three partners, who all had worked in the same group for IBM in Kansas City, had heard of me. In our contact, I was told that they were considering a business start-up designing, assembling, and selling ticketing printers to airlines. They realized it would be challenging, and they asked me to assess each of them in terms of their management potential and to give each one individual feedback. Then they wanted me to meet collectively with the three of them as they decided if and how they wanted to form a partnership. I can't remember the content of our discussions, but I was impressed with the competence and the openness in our meetings. Ultimately, two partners decided not to go forward with the venture, leaving Dean Lawrence as the sole owner.

Lawrence was highly intelligent and knowledgeable about the printer in which he collaborated on designing. He also was confident, a person who always seemed to emerge as the leader of groups with which he was associated. He understood the IBM sales model, and he had personal experience in the field, meeting with users both in airlines and in travel agencies.

With his technical knowledge, he could design and modify printers for specific applications. He could train a sales staff and order entry groups. He built a staff of mostly female telephone sales solicitors and order takers. Products made and assembled by an outside vender were state of the art and initially in heavy demand. Lawrence represented sole management. Everyone else performed specific task functions, primarily in sales. Most of the sales representatives were adept at their trade and formed close working relationships with their customers. Lawrence was an avid skier. He and one of his associates worked for several years trying to create a customer-actuated lift ticket dispenser, to no avail.

The company was small, but it had a list of the top airlines as customers. The company was profitable for years, but the market was getting increasingly competitive. The business was not large enough to sustain a consulting psychologist, but Lawrence and I were friends, and I was often around like a kitchen cabinet member. As competitive technology emerged, Lawrence sold the company, and I lost contact with him.

Robert (Bob) Wagner, Marsh & McLennan Management (Marsh Mac)

Bob Wagner was a highly intelligent, socially impressive entrepreneur. His meteoric rise through the IBM ranks made him a prime target for recruiters, and he was selected to become president and CEO of Waddell & Reed, an investment adviser in Overland Park, Kansas, listed on the New York Stock Exchange.

I only met Wagner through a mutual friend after he left Waddell & Reed to join Marsh & McLennan, the country's largest business insurance broker, as president of a newly created management services consulting division in Kansas City. Marsh Mac was interested in expanding into management consulting.

Wagner was starting from scratch with only an administrative staff. He was spending time in the New York headquarters office, finalizing a plan in which insurance consultants from Marsh Mac offices around the country would locate projects and open doors for the management consultants. I spent time both consulting with Wagner and interviewing prospective candidates, including known affiliates from IBM and Waddell & Reed. Wagner was intent on using the IBM model of hiring an impressive sales force with strong technical backup. Although I interviewed several candidates, none were hired for the Kansas City office.

Wagner also tried to recruit me as the corporate psychologist for Marsh Management with the plan of developing clients through Marsh Mac's insurance consultants. I thanked Wagner and explained why I didn't think his model would work. A former client, R. B. Jones and Company, a national brokerage competitor of Marsh Mac, had once considered a program like Bob Wagner's program. Existing brokerage agents were to be used to open doors for consultants selling new services. The program failed. A business insurance salesman with a longtime hip-pocket account was not about to jeopardize his meal ticket.

I knew Wagner had a tough task ahead of him. He was keeping busy doing some consulting for the Marsh Mac corporate group, but he didn't hire any of the people I interviewed for him. Our relationship, and I think Wagner's project, just seemed to fade away.

Ironically, at the turn of the century, Marsh Mac formed an HR division that acquired several organizations that provided management consulting services, including the Delta Consulting Group. Today Marsh has a full-fledged management consulting group performing at a level comparable to McKinsey and the Boston Consulting Group.

Comments

Business Men's Assurance Company (BMA), a major insurance company controlled by three generations of the Grant family, was an outstanding long-term client. Quasi-monopolistic insurance arrangements provided a strong draw for competent talent, managed by Ken Higdon and Bill Sayler, in their respective roles as president. The focus of Bill

Grant as CEO was directed toward noninsurance diversified investments, community involvement, and philanthropy. BMA was able to provide career support to employees through most of the downturn in the economy.

Some impressive entrepreneurial models emerge in this section. Jim Barickman created a major national advertising agency that maximizes his social skills in acquiring and retaining clients while also structuring an operation in which he monitored daily activity.

If ever the proverb "Necessity is the mother of invention" were valid, it would certainly apply to Walter W. Ross. His creation of Beta Sigma Phi International in 1931 during the depths of the Depression was an amazing accomplishment.

Bill Merrick, the managing partner of Arthur Young & Company (AY) was so involved with the development of his staff, he built a reputation whereby he could replenish his staff vacancies each year with the top accounting students graduating from the University of Alabama.

Pat Willingham, one of the top students who joined AY, headed management services. He developed and invested in medical enterprises, and he eventually served as owner/CEO of a medical company providing services throughout Alabama and Mississippi.

R. B. Jones, an old-line, major broker of commercial insurance, created a quasi-monopolistic edge with captive accounts and by servicing the business of major producers.

Jim O'Crowley, with an outstanding corporate background, marketed himself as a turnaround specialist with one of the most poignant marketing letters I have ever read.

Forrest Jones, with the help of his wife, Dottie, literally created a career through a dedicated commitment to self-improvement. He went from a career selling insurance supplies to agents on commission, to his purchase with Dottie of a small insurance agency in Kansas City selling insurance and financial products to associations. The company grew dramatically.

CHAPTER SIX

RESTAURANTS

E arly in my career I had the good fortune of running into an old acquaintance, Richard J. (Rick) Harman, a person with such a sterling reputation that his endorsement alone created for me a strong presence in the restaurant industry. He was a rare person whose friendship I cherish.

The National Restaurant Association was founded in Kansas City by Myron Green, the grandfather of Harman's wife, Susanne. The city has a tradition of having outstanding restaurants with civic-minded owners. Harman perpetuated that image.

Richard J. Harman, Myron Green Restaurants

Rick Harman was an outstanding person who also happened to have built an outstanding cafeteria and restaurant organization. He was one of the most positive people I have ever known. Once he believed in something, he could sell it to anyone. His sincerity was beyond question. He was instrumental in expanding my career as a psychological consultant after I had started consulting with his company, Myron Green Cafeterias. Over a short period, he "sold" me to a half dozen of his friends who were owners, presidents, or managers with authority to hire me.

This memoir provides me with an opportunity to acknowledge Rick's impact on my life as a friend and supporter. He was a rare and inspirational leader.

The opening statement of his obituary in 2010 was succinct: "If there ever was a man that always saw the donut, never the hole, it was Rick Harman."

What follows is an excerpt from Harman's obituary:

> An All-State athlete at Hoisington, Kansas, high school; Big man on campus at Kansas State University; all Big 7 basketball forward in 1949; All-American in 1950; President of Beta Theta Pi fraternity; Student Council president senior year; Married to Susanne Green, 1949; 1950-53, Air Force Captain; 1953, began career in restaurant industry with father-in-law at Myron Green Cafeterias; President of both Missouri and National Restaurant Associations; Republican standard bearer for Kansas governor in 1968; U.S. Olympic committee in 1974; Kansas City Rotary president, host in 1985 for the International Convention in Kansas City; 1990s, Kansas Board of Regents, where he advocated for universal educational opportunities, focusing on expansion of junior colleges and satellite campuses . . .
>
> All-State, All-American, All-Everything: His accomplishments are too numerous to cover. Rick never lost his curiosity to dream and constantly challenged convention with

the "why nots" and "what ifs"; he was one of the top Kansas citizens of this generation.

Harman and I had our first contact in December 1950 at the Big Seven annual preseason basketball tournament held in Kansas City. He played for Kansas State, and I played for the University of Colorado. He was a six-foot, three-inch senior, all-conference forward, and I was a five-foot, ten-inch sophomore, reserve guard. We were also members of the same fraternity, Beta Theta Pi. Our next contact was in March 1952, when we played together on an all-star basketball team that was assembled after the Air Force championship tournament.

Our next contact was close to ten years later at the Kansas University (KU) relays. I had finished a master's degree at CU and a Ph.D. at KU. I had married Rena, a graduate of Kansas State (K-State), and I had started my career in Kansas City as a consulting management psychologist with enough confidence to talk about it. Harman was by himself. As we sat down, we recognized each other. Rena and Rick were at K-State at the same time. We talked K-State, the highlights of the relays, and then he asked me about my work. When he left, he asked me to call him.

Myron Green, Rick's grandfather-in-law, a dentist more interested in business than dentistry, opened the Myron Green Cafeteria in Kansas City in 1909. He subsequently opened two more cafeterias and started a contract feeding operation. He was visionary in creating the Kansas City Business Men's Association that grew into the National Restaurant Association, started in Kansas City in 1919 with Myron Green as its founding president. Harman's father-in-law, Watson Green, was more of a traditional businessman. The holdings had been reduced to one cafeteria in downtown Kansas City, Missouri, that was blessed with a few long-term female employees who oversaw both the administration and the operation.

Watson Green was gracious in granting Rick Harman autonomous rein in managing the operation. Harman opened a second cafeteria in the Kansas City suburb of Mission, Kansas, hiring an outstanding woman who managed the cafeteria and ultimately became the company's operations manager. Harman also started a contract feeding division, providing in-house luncheon service to companies owned by business friends and contacts, and a gourmet restaurant on the state line between Missouri and Kansas.

In our first meeting, Harman decided quickly that he wanted to use me to assess his key people, and we established a time for me to interview him. Harman was very intelligent. He had been an excellent student. Ideas and plans of action seemed to pop into his head. He dealt in broad concepts, and he hated to get bogged down in detail. He knew clearly what he wanted to do and what he didn't want to do. His personal makeup seemed perfect for being what he always had been, "All Everything."

He understood clearly what he wanted to do with Myron Green. He wanted to hire competent people to run his organization so that he could do what he was best at—making contacts, bringing in business, and coming up with ideas. From his first day with Myron Green, Harman knew what he would not do. Harman would never pick up a plate or try to gain expertise in the areas in which he had already hired experts.

When I interviewed his key people, I recognized that he generally had excellent people who were effective in the positions they held. There were no crisis situations, and I didn't see a need for a routine relationship. Rather, Harman and I established a friend/consultant relationship where I provided ad hoc interviews of interesting people he met that might fit into a present or future business relationship.

Harman was almost like an old prospector looking for gold nuggets. The person he met would have explained something of his or her past work history, either factual or embellished. Harman generally would accept the person's statement at face value, but with his optimism, he would also hypothesize that beyond the surface was a gold nugget waiting to emerge.

We had a good understanding, and I saved Harman a lot of time by screening his prospects. Harman, of course, also did come up with some outstanding gold nuggets, including his daughter Betsy and her husband Ed Holland, who became the general managers, and ultimately, the owners of Myron Green. With Rick Harman's assistance in bringing new business, Myron Green grew to an organization of forty-nine facilities, including three restaurants and cafeterias in Kansas City and thirteen in St. Louis, as well as contract feeding facilities serving companies, nursing homes, and youth homes markets around the country.

Harman was a humanistic person. He had a strong drive to help people, both individually and through his political activities and his commitments to the Missouri and National Restaurant Associations, the Kansas Board of Regents, Rotary, and other countless organizations with which he was associated. Harman was an activist in fighting discrimination wherever he found it. Having a cafeteria in Missouri with Jim Crow laws during the 1950s and early 1960s was a conflict for him that he fought through the restaurant associations.

In 1968 when Harman was running for governor as a Republican against a Democratic incumbent, he asked me to serve on the program committee, suggesting that I could bring up ideas about social change. I arrived enthusiastically for the meeting, but I left fifteen minutes later. I learned that the function of the program committee was to make sure that there were no new programs. If he had won, Harman would have made a great governor. He would have selected capable people and given them backing.

National Restaurant Association

Peter Drucker observed many years ago that associations are among the weakest of organizations because it is so difficult to hold the operating management accountable. A new president is elected from the membership every year, and board members generally have variable levels of expertise with contradictory agendas.

Rick Harman devoted a lot of time and frustration to the National Restaurant Association. Prior to beginning his year as president, the former senior staff CEO left. Harman was responsible for selecting the new CEO, and he had selected a young Ph.D. from one of the top hotel and restaurant programs who had some management experience along with his academic credentials. He asked me to assess him. From a psychological perspective, he was outstanding with potential to grow. He was young and lacked leadership experience, but with Harman's optimism, I knew he would be hired.

Harman also hired me as a consultant to the National Restaurant Association. During his term as president, I provided assessments and feedbacks to the key association management and professional staff. I spent time discussing each person I assessed with the new CEO.

On each visit, a sizable block of my time was made available to the CEO. At the end of my engagement, I felt satisfied that the National Restaurant Association staff consisted of individuals with capabilities compatible with the expectations in their job descriptions. The new CEO had a mission statement and an understanding of strengths, weaknesses, and developmental needs of his staff in meeting accountabilities.

Although I treated the assignment as if I were working with a client, I saw it as a project. The CEO seemed appreciative and positive about my involvement, but I couldn't imagine that anyone I assessed felt comfortable having someone in their midst reporting to the membership's president.

Follow-up information from Harman after my project ended validated our concern about the CEO's inexperience. He did run into resistance from some staff complaints to influential members, but he performed his job successfully for several years. When he left, it was for a better business opportunity.

As president, Harman probably made a greater contribution to the National Restaurant Association than any of his predecessors. He quickly understood a problem and created a meaningful strategy for addressing it—what he did throughout his life.

Worker Attitude Inventory

With his positive outlook, Rick always saw ways to successful outcomes without becoming bogged down with barriers, even when advising friends, or in my case, his psychologist. Working as a clinical psychologist at the Veteran's Administration Center in Leavenworth, Kansas, I did a research study on the hiring of entry-level food service workers for the Federal civil service commission. Their problem arose from an inability to hire anyone based on the standard intellectual test in use. My approach was to develop a hypothetical model of the "ideal" food service worker.[13]

The 168-item Worker Attitude Inventory (WAI), a true-false inventory, was constructed logically to measure the expected responses of ideal employees. The median age of the group was 44, and the median grade attended in school was the ninth grade.

The hypothesis that a positive relationship existed between ratings on the WAI and supervisory ratings was supported for the total group at the .01 level of confidence. Although I gave the test to employees at both a Myron Green cafeteria and a Putsch's cafeteria, I viewed the WAI as a research tool and not part of a commercial undertaking.

Harman saw immediate commercial applications and told me he could line up most of the members of the National Restaurant Association. I thought of the problems that I might have and decided not to go forward with his idea. Today I recognize my past personal and professional inexperience and continue to admire and respect Harman's judgment.

The Management of People in Hotels, Restaurants, and Clubs

A small group of consultants to the National Restaurant Association held informal meetings each year prior to the start of the annual trade show. I was invited to give a talk at one of the meetings about my research on the role of successful food service workers.

One of the attendees was Donald E. (Don) Lundberg, head of the University of Connecticut Hotel & Restaurant Management School and a prolific author of information relative to the industry. Lundberg had published a small personnel management manual, and he realized a need for a professional management book. He proposed that we collaborate on a book in which he would provide information relevant to the industry and I would provide psychologically relevant management material. *The Management of People in Hotels, Restaurants and Clubs*, by Donald E. Lundberg and James P. Armatas (four editions), was the leading textbook for hotel and restaurant management schools for over twenty years.

Missouri Restaurant Association

With his involvement in the Missouri Restaurant Association, Harman encouraged my volunteer involvement, both to help the association and to build my reputation. In 1961, the University of Missouri introduced its first course in restaurant management under Jack Welch, a retired executive and son of one of the founders of the National Restaurant Association.

Prior to Welch's involvement, Kansas City and St. Louis each had its own trade association. The Missouri Restaurant Association was nonfunctional. Welch was a zealot, determined to make his mark in upgrading the restaurant industry. Harman was Welch's primary supporter. In 1962, the Kansas City and St. Louis associations agreed to affiliate as chapters of the Missouri Restaurant Association, marking the true birth of the association. Welch zeroed in on any resources available, and I presented several management workshops.

Through Harman's efforts, my name became known in the restaurant industry, and he encouraged the Four Winds restaurant, owned by William (Joe) Joseph Gilbert and William (Bill) Joseph Gilbert Jr., and Putsch's restaurants, owned by Justice (Jud) Putsch, to use me. From my contributions to the Missouri Restaurant Association, I was involved in several projects in Kansas City and St. Louis involving ad hoc assessments and training seminars. My coauthor, Don Lundberg, left the University of Connecticut to start a new hotel/restaurant program at California State Polytechnic University in Pomona, California. I did a few workshops and lectures for Lundberg.

Paul Robinson, Gilbert-Robinson

Prior to the 1970s, Kansas City was the only major city with a downtown airport. Landing from the east was always a heart-stopping experience, waiting to pass over the downtown tall buildings before diving toward the runway. Joe Gilbert, the son-in-law of George Fowler, one of the contemporaries of Myron Green, opened the Four Winds restaurant in 1940. The restaurant, within the airport, was leased from the city for $10 per year. Bill Gilbert joined his dad in 1945 after returning from service during World War II.

Rick Harman recommended me to the Gilberts, and I started a consulting relationship that entailed a pattern of dramatic growth. Harman not only introduced me to the Gilberts but also introduced the Gilberts to the dramatic growth plan they were to follow.

For its total existence, the Four Winds was one of the finest restaurants in Kansas City, with an excellent chef, quality food, excellent service, and a standard procedure in which each plate leaving the kitchen was inspected by one of the managers. It was a perfect situation for the Gilberts, one that they had never thought of changing. Bill Gilbert, who remained a friend and fellow member of a country club in La Quinta, California, once said that I had changed his life in my psychological feedback session when I asked him what he planned to do with his life.

Bill Gilbert didn't have much time to ponder the question I raised for two reasons. The first involved a newly elected mayor and city council in Kansas City with plans to reassign airport leases, and the second involved the formation of a task force to plan for a new airport.

Rick Harman had a high regard for the Gilberts and for a person named Paul Robinson, who was general manager of the Golden Ox, a nationally recognized steak house in Kansas City's West Bottoms that was owned by the Stockyards Company. The Stockyards owned the Golden Ox, but Paul Robinson had 100 percent accountability for the total operation. Harman proposed to the Gilberts that he, they, and Paul Robinson form a company to develop new restaurants. Harman scheduled me to assess Paul Robinson.

Robinson was a free-spirited person with longer hair and more casual attire than the typical manager of that era. He attributed his management outlook to the first general manager of the Golden Ox, whom Robinson admired as one of the most creative people he knew. The Golden Ox represented the country's first concept steak house that could compete directly with a prime French restaurant. Whereas a French restaurant had to bear the cost and accoutrements of a French chef, Paul could train his dishwasher to fry a steak, put it on a big platter with a baked potato, provide a big salad on the side, and charge as much as the French restaurant.

Robinson was obviously intelligent and creative—an outstanding management prospect. All I could do was reaffirm what others close to him knew and Rick Harman suspected.

Although Harman put the plan together, he could not become a part of the plan. Prior to visualizing the plan, Myron Green invested in a newly created concept chicken operation and opened two restaurants in Johnson County, Kansas, a Kansas City suburb. Unfortunately, the operations did not fare well and eventually failed.

The rest is history. Guided by Paul Robinson's creative genius, Gilbert-Robinson became one of the great American restaurant growth stories. They started in 1962 with a new steak house, the Inn at the Landing shopping center, then opened the Plaza III Steakhouse at the Country Club Plaza, both in Kansas City, Missouri. Both restaurants were overwhelming successes.

Although the Golden Ox was nationally recognized, the physical facility was old and rustic. The new facilities designed by Paul Robinson were elegant in style, decor, and service. Robinson and Bill Gilbert both assumed general management roles.

With his creative vision, Robinson spent most of his time in staff-type roles, planning and working on decor concepts. Once a plan was in place, he expected general managers reporting to him to follow his strict guidelines. I learned firsthand about Robinson's operating style.

One of my good friends from high school in Denver was Horace (Bud) Hawkins, a highly intelligent, highly independent person. He had started working in resort restaurants while in high school, quickly earning a reputation as being a natural and a leader with creative ideas. He parlayed his experience into opening a popular restaurant in Denver, funded by an investment group. It was ideal for his ego needs but not for his financial needs.

When the Plaza III was ready to open and a search for a general manager was initiated, I mentioned Hawkins's name. My formal assessment read a lot like my assessment on Paul Robinson. Hawkins was hired, but conflict between Hawkins and Robinson was inevitable and Hawkins was terminated early in his employment. There was no question of Robinson's strong leadership and what he expected from operating managers reporting to him. Incidentally, I never again suggested an acquaintance to a client.

In 1972, another of Paul Robinson's creations, Houlihan's, launched. Mary Gibson, a former management employee, described Houlihan's in the *Kansas City Business Journal* as

> A truly groundbreaking restaurant concept. Before Paul Robinson began designing restaurants, casual dining was usually without style or imagination . . . He was a great gentleman and intensely creative. He taught a whole generation of young restauranteurs the importance of restaurant design and creating concepts that were fresh and appealing.

Robinson was able to envision great concepts in mundane settings. The first Houlihan's restaurant was in the Country Club Plaza in a space previously housing Houlihan's Men's Wear. With a play on words, Paul had a perfect name—Houlihan's Old Place!

During the Gilbert-Robinson era, the Kansas City Plaza shopping center, owned by the J. C. Nichols Company, was recognized as one of the first and most outstanding shopping centers in the country. The only way a restaurant could open on the Plaza was by invitation. To ensure the quality of its tenants, Nichols had a graduated rental scale, subsidizing new start-ups but taking a sizable percent from the gross income of successful operations.

The Country Club Plaza was the primary venue for introducing the many successful concept restaurants created by Paul Robinson, most of which were expanded nationally. In addition to Houlihan's, Paul created Fred P. Ott's, Annie's Santa Fe, and Bristol's Bar & Grill.

In preparing a real estate project modeled after the J. C. Nichols Company, Del Dunmire interviewed a former Nichols employee who managed the Country Club Plaza. All Gilbert-Robinson properties were extremely popular and paid top rental dollars.

One of Robinson's most creative concept restaurants that opened in a suburban shopping center was closed after a few months at a serious loss. The restaurant catered to children and their parents, who used the restaurant to throw birthday parties for other children and their parents. The experience was so delightful, the restaurant was quickly booked in advance. Unfortunately, the experience was so good for the children they wouldn't leave. There was no turnover and, therefore, no profit!

I was instrumental in working closely with Robinson and Gilbert in the early days of the company, but the company grew quickly with new investors and new executives and my involvement ended. Houlihan's alone expanded to eighty-four locations in eighteen states; 60 percent of the restaurants were franchised. My involvement was limited to the Kansas City operations prior to their national expansion.

The company went public in 1976 and was sold to W. R. Grace, a conglomerate, in 1978. Paul Robinson died in 2010 at the age of eighty-seven. Bill Gilbert died in 2017 at the age of ninety-four.

Justice (Jud) Putsch, Putsch's Restaurants

For most of its history, Putsch's consisted of three distinct restaurants, all within one block of one another in the Country Club Plaza in Kansas City, one of the first and finest suburban shopping centers in the country. Born in 1909, Jud Putsch spent his teenage years working in the family cafeteria in Kansas City, developing a distaste for the restaurant business. He graduated from the University of Missouri and earned a master's degree from Harvard Business School in 1931.

He joined the executive training program at R. H. Macy & Co. in New York, set on a career in merchandising. He spent the next nine years working for a Macy's affiliate in New Jersey, steadily working his way up the corporate ladder.

Putsch returned to Kansas City in 1940 after his mother died suddenly and his father became ill. He and his wife, Virginia, ran the family cafeteria for two years until he went into the Navy during World War II. Virginia Putsch kept the cafeteria going until the couple sold it in 1944.

The couple returned to the restaurant business in 1947 when they opened Putsch's 210 on the Country Club Plaza. Featuring continental cuisine, elegant decor, and a string trio, Putsch's 210 was the premier restaurant in Kansas City in the 1950s and 1960s, and in fact, one of the best restaurants in the country west of the Mississippi. The Putschs opened two more restaurants on the Plaza in the 1950s and 1960s—Putsch's Cafeteria and Putsch's Coffee Shop. Each successfully catered to a different style of dining, a rare achievement in the restaurant business. Putsch later opened the first sidewalk café on the Plaza, an extension of the coffee shop. They also expanded their cafeterias into suburban areas in Kansas and Missouri.

Jud and Virginia Putsch made an ideal partnership. He always considered himself to be in the merchandising business, and she paid tenacious attention to everyday detail. Whatever the business, it had to be the absolute best in terms of concept, appearance, and delivery. What-ever the product or the price, it had to be of the highest quality and presentation. In his planning for the 210, Jud Putsch spent months researching elegant New York restaurants, concentrating on only the finest features of each and getting menu items down to perfection.

At least thirty-five years after Putsch's 210 closed, the following remem-brance appeared in *The Pitch*, a Kansas City trade publication, under the title of "Remembering Putsch's 210":

> I remember the fantastic gold service—the best of every-thing in Kansas City. Everything was wheeled on cart, ta-bleside, and finished at the table. They served all the famous flaming desserts: Crepes suzette, Cherries jubilee, Bananas Foster. There was also a strolling violinist, Louis Cina, who wandered from table to table while a pianist accompanied him on a grand piano located in a little niche . . .

> It was all very elegant, sort of New York City supper club sophisticated. Most Kansas Citians wouldn't know how to behave in a place like that today . . . My favorite entrees were the curried shrimp and the shrimp creole and I loved the condiments of corn relish and watermelon rind served in a sterling silver relish container with the salads, which were prepared tableside."

The next restaurant to open was the cafeteria, which was considered be-cause a large space was available around the corner from the 210 with space under the street for consolidating kitchens, administration, and storage needs for both facilities. The planning and construction for the cafeteria took a year, establishing layout, securing equipment, setting up menus, and testing recipes.

Staff were hired early, trained thoroughly, and prepared to make opening day look routine. Putsch was always concerned that all restaurants, regardless of age, should appear to be newly opened with all furniture, fixtures, and equipment looking new. He always remodeled a year before necessary.

In opening a cafeteria, Jud and Virginia Putsch were operating in familiar territory. Their cafeterias were outstanding from the start. Managers were well trained through on-the-job experience and skilled hourly workers were in abundance in Kansas City.

There were no outstanding coffee shops in Kansas City. Coffee shops were a California innovation. When they decided to open a coffee shop, they knew they needed a model to follow. It was decided that the top coffee shop in America was Marie Callender's. Two Putsch managers who were to manage the Putsch coffee shop were sent to California to secure positions in management with Marie Callender's and to document all policies and procedures. Returning to Kansas City, they provided the Putsch organization with a systematic plan for initiating a new, highly profitable operation.

With foresight and planning, Jud Putsch created a unique organization, capable of creating extreme profitability. Three top restaurants in a prime Kansas City shopping center were served by one shared administrative/operations center. Expenses were reduced dramatically. The organization also added profitable cafeterias selectively into suburban locations.

Marcor

The Putschs sold their organization in 1971 to Marcor, with headquarters in Chicago. But Marcor did not take control of the company until 1976. During this interim period, Virginia Putsch, who had been in failing health, disengaged from the company; Jud Putsch kept the title of president but served more as an adviser. General manager Bruce McMullin took on broader responsibilities.

McMullin was hired as general manager in 1967. He had a background as a country club manager in Little Rock, Arkansas. He had made an outstanding contribution with the Putsch organization, and he was the obvious choice to succeed Jud Putsch. He became president when Marcor assumed operational control.

Marcor was a holding of Montgomery Ward that owned diverse chains of restaurants when they also added the Putsch organization. Their plan was to achieve national growth. Although Marcor did not take operational control, the president of Marcor held regular meetings with McMullin and Jud Putsch. Putsch's 210 apparently did not fit into their growth model and closed in 1973. The rest of the Putsch organization continued doing well financially, and I was involved with providing management development training in anticipation of future expansion when Marcor took operational control.

At the time of its acquisition by Marcor in 1971, the Putsch organization recognized that its current centralized organizational structure was not conducive to optimal growth. Although the management structure was not altered at that time, a major decision was made relative to the hiring practices of management trainees and assistant managers. No longer would individuals be hired to fill slots, but each candidate was considered on his/her potential to become an independently functioning unit manager or higher.

By the start of 1975, a major reorganizational decision was made that involved the establishment of a decentralized organizational structure with the unit manager taking on greater independent responsibility. Two preliminary steps were of critical importance: (1) a centralized system was needed in areas of finance, quality assurance, and personnel and (2) the management development program was to include management by objectives (MBO) training. Ultimate success of MBO depended on the development of meaningful company-wide financial information and controls.

In the book I coauthored with Don Lundberg, I described a reorganizational program undertaken in anticipation of the strategic reorganization of Putsch's once the Marcor acquisition was initiated. In 1976, on alternate weeks, a ten-session, three-hours per session training program was initiated that was developed and conducted by me.[14]

In 1976, without prior warning, Marcor filed for chapter 7 bankruptcy. The factors leading to the abrupt and ultimate demise of the Putsch group in 1976 are unclear. In 1976 Marcor became a privately held company. At least one of the Putsch executives was permitted to invest in the new ownership. Shortly thereafter, a bankruptcy closed the Putsch organization and its operations, all of which had shown consistent profitability.

Although Marcor must have paid a fortune to have acquired the Putsch restaurants in 1971, to my knowledge there was no attempt to sell any of the units or to continue operations. Bruce McMullin finished his career as general manager of the Indian Hills Country Club in Mission Hills, Kansas.

The Marcor episode was so confusing, my post hoc analysis came up with the following information: Marcor was formed in 1968 through a merger of a struggling Montgomery Ward with the Container Corporation of America. Mobil Oil bought Marcor in 1974 and subsequently bought Montgomery Ward in 1976.

Comments

My father and my older brother, Nick, spent their lives in the restaurant/bar business. My other older brother, Phil, spent the early part of his career in the restaurant bar/business before getting a Ph.D. in clinical psychology and ending up as the chief psychologist at the VA Hospital in Kansas City. During high school and some of my college years, I worked part-time in my father's restaurant/bar, but I decided early that the restaurant business was not for me. I recognized the hard work, time demand, and risks facing a restaurant entrepreneur.

Through my relationship with Rick Harman, I realized how ironic it was that people were looking to me for advice in a field I shunned. I also gained tremendous respect for successful entrepreneurs in a field in which most entrepreneurs were failures. Looking back on the advice Harvey Thomas gave me that my clients would train me, I learned a lot from people I interviewed.

I remembered early in my career going to a newly opened restaurant in Kansas City reportedly funded by a group of physicians and lawyers. The food and the ambiance were both outstanding, and the restaurant was packed. A few days after my visit, I interviewed a midlevel applicant for one of my client companies. I commented about the restaurant to the candidate, and he said, "They will be out of business in a couple of months." He said they didn't have capable management. In his visit, he recognized waiters he described as a gang of thieves who would "steal them blind." Two months later, they were out of business.

Compare that restaurant with the Putsch organization. Elaborate financial controls were in place. Kitchens, supplies, warehouses, and administrative areas were in a belowground space by which all entry and exit access was controlled through a door thirty inches wide with a stern lady sitting at the door—ready to investigate the contents of anything coming in or leaving the building. All successful restaurants must control shrinkage before they do anything else.

The three managers described in this chapter were outstanding individuals with outstanding reputations. Rick Harman was a rare person, possessing many of the traits we ideally hope are present in our politicians but rarely come through. Harman was the real thing. He built a large, profitable business on his reputation for honesty and leadership. What he needed were competent people to implement his leadership, which he found in his own family.

Jud Putsch showed a high degree of perfection in all aspects of his enterprise. The strength of his operation was in consolidating all facets into a predictable, controllable, monopolistic enterprise that generated extreme profits with controllable expense. There is something to be learned by Marcor's poor judgment in investing in an enterprise that did not fit its own model for expansion.

Paul Robinson, as recognized by Rick Harman, was a creative genius who was able to parlay his talent into remarkable accomplishments.

Although his focus forced him away from operations, he was clearly in charge and not likely to lose a power struggle.

CHAPTER SEVEN

MANUFACTURING COMPANIES

Manufacturing companies were my favorite clients.

As a psychologist training and working in Veteran's Administration hospitals, I knew little about manufacturing, but I understood organizational structure and bureaucratic inefficiency. I worked in a chronic hospital environment in a time of impending change, and my mission was not to fit in. It was to challenge the environment, even if the bureaucracy was resistive to change. I also had the organizational development tools necessary to assist in bringing about change.

My first management consulting project was with the Hoerner Box Company, a manufacturer of corrugated boxes. In my interviews, I had standard questions related to the enjoyable aspects of the job and the not-so-enjoyable problem areas. I quickly discovered that there are so many moving parts in a manufacturing company that problems are easy to identify. I also discovered that Hoerner management and subsequent manufacturing and mining management companies with which I consulted were eager for change.

My early contact with Colt Industries introduced me to the Fairbanks Morse Pump Company, my most instructive and long-term consulting assignment. With Colt Industries I also had long-term consulting assignments with two divisions of the Central Moloney Electric Company and three divisions of Menasco, Inc.

Without question, the many years spent with Colt Industries, Growth Industries, Puritan-Bennett, the Drummond Company, and my own manufacturing company, Alvarado Manufacturing Company, were the most professionally rewarding experiences in my career.

Parker B. Francis, Puritan-Bennett & Company

Puritan-Bennett was founded in Kansas City, Missouri, in 1913 by Parker B. Francis, a creative and domineering person, as a manufacturer and distributor of oxygen and hydrogen. Through the systematic efforts of Francis, the company created a near monopoly in gases and equipment sold to industrial, medical, and aeronautical users by setting up a network of national dealers able to fill cylinders within their own geographic locations.

In the 1950s, Francis created another near monopoly. The company entered the medical equipment field with the acquisition of the Bennett Company in Santa Monica, California. Bennett was the inventor of a mechanical ventilator as an alternative to the iron lung machine. In the 1960s, the introduction of the MA-1 volume ventilator brought Puritan-Bennett to the forefront of the medical market with a ventilator that assisted a patient's breathing and controlled respiration should the patient stop breathing. John F. Kennedy died on a Bennett respirator.

In 1956, Parker B. Francis turned the business over to his sons—Parker B. Francis III and John B. Francis—creating internal problems with Parker Francis, aggressive, domineering, and impulsive, as CEO and John Francis, reserved and conservative as chairman. The dynamics within the Francis family had a profound effect on various outcomes in the company. John Francis was intimidated easily and hesitant to become involved with conflict. Parker Francis could disrupt whole departments with his impulsive, often irrational, demands. The roles of insiders, particularly Thurman (Thurm) Erickson, vice president of industrial relations, were critical in cleaning up problems and mediating conflict. All hiring decisions were made unilaterally under Erickson's authority. The company was blessed with loyal, competent managers, and a strong human resource function was quick to identify and react to problem issues.

One of Erickson's impressive accomplishments was the elimination of the unions, thus ensuring operational stability and continuity. Erickson kept the company lean. Job descriptions were accurate, and power struggles were minimal.

I started my consulting relationship with Puritan-Bennett in the early 1970s during the period of rapid growth and earnings. Erickson knew of me and contacted me. I reported directly to Erickson, and my contacts involved him and various department heads with which I had ad hoc assessment assignments.

Thurm Erickson was a true professional. Unbeknownst to me, he ran a one-year research project correlating my assessment predictions with actual performance. Fortunately, the results were positive for my performance, which solidified my role with the company.

Parker Francis's wife was a beautiful woman who had a cardiac arrest while undergoing cosmetic surgery in the early 1970s and was kept alive on a Bennett ventilator. With the tragedy, Parker Francis disengaged from the company. He built a large electrified fence around his house in Kansas City and flew with his wife to Chicago every week in a private plane for some esoteric treatment. He had a male aide who, with his son, served as caretakers. I rarely had contact with Parker Francis in the company, but I did witness his soft side. He summoned me with a request to "test" the son of the caretaker. Francis wanted to send him to college, but he wanted me to tell him if the son was college material. The son did not do well on tests, but I did my best to convince Parker that the son had the stability and discipline to succeed in college.

I did not learn the denouement of Parker Francis's struggles, but he decided to retire and not return to the company. A conciliatory CEO, Owen Pinkerman, a former hospital administrator, was selected as his replacement. I was not involved with Pinkerman's hiring, but he was a hands-off leader—the antithesis of Parker Francis. Pinkerman delegated totally to those in charge and was supportive in following through on requests. He was supportive of my involvement in the company.

The company grew rapidly. The parent company reorganized itself as the Puritan-Bennett Corporation and consolidated its medical marketing department into a single unit in Overland Park, Kansas. The volume ventilators were manufactured in a 500,000-square-foot facility in Santa Monica, California. Puritan Equipment in Lenexa, Kansas, made small fittings and plug-ins for oxygen and nitrous oxide for hospitals and doctor's offices, and oxygen systems for small private jets.

The company was willing to experiment in multiple directions, including entrée into the home health care market. After purchasing several home health care distributorships, the company formed a new marketing department under the name Medical with modest success.

Thurm Erickson retired in the 1970s. He was not replaced, creating a serious lack of central control. Most operating areas were staffed with competent people. Human resources under J. W. Jones and George Laddish still had stature gained through Erickson's leadership.

Most of the successful companies with which I was involved had strong leadership in setting direction and ensuring accountability of operating areas. Puritan-Bennett was unique in that John Francis and Owen Pinkerman delegated considerable autonomy to line managership. Puritan-Bennett, except for the medical marketing group, was a small company with experienced, organized mid-managers performing predictable tasks.

I consulted with Puritan-Bennett for approximately ten years. My role with the company evolved slowly. Rather than being engaged by top management, I was directed by the HR executives who scheduled me to assess candidates and promising midlevel employees, slowly introducing me to key management. Over time my role broadened with full company acceptance, including regular meetings with John Francis and Owen Pinkerman, who by then viewed me as an important resource for the company.

Medical Marketing

My primary commitment was to the medical marketing group. Under the initial leadership of Guy Woodliff, the sales functions went through a major overhaul. Woodliff had a successful career in medical equipment management. In joining Puritan-Bennett, he quickly set up regional offices to oversee the activities of sales representatives in sixty territories in America and Canada. I was instrumental in assessing existing sales representatives and all new sales candidates. Woodliff was oriented strongly to show results, and he brought in key corporate management staff, started formal training programs, and developed formal marketing strategies and incentive programs.

He also had some cleaning up to do. Along with the sixty sales territories, he inherited two health care units, leftovers from the Medical disaster. The oversight was being handled by a midlevel administrator in the marketing group. One day when I walked into Woodliff's office, he clapped his hands and told me that he had sold the health care units.

The program quickly blossomed under Woodliff and continued to grow under his successor, Russell (Russ) Pennavaria. Under Pennavaria, I undertook a major project identifying the characteristics of high- and low-producing salesmen by evaluating past psychological assessments, psychological testing profiles, and present performance descriptions made by regional managers. It was an extensive project, depicting hypothetical models of individuals likely to succeed or show low performance with Puritan-Bennett. A summary of the implications of the study is as follows:

> Skill in working with others seems to be critical. Successful Puritan-Bennett salesmen not only are able to sell and conduct group training sessions, they greatly enjoy the satisfaction and personal recognition they receive from such activities. In selecting inexperienced people in the future, a key should lie in the skill and comfort they show in interpersonal roles and in their receptivity to direction and supervision.
>
> Puritan-Bennett is a structured organization in which sales freedom can be granted only within defined parameters.

Highly independent, individualistic salesmen do not fit well nor show productivity. A major requirement of salesmen is the ability to do paperwork and to show facility with written communications.

The criteria being used at present in selecting salesmen seem to have some validity. High intelligence and/or considerable specific product and field knowledge seem to be essential. Successful sales experience within the medical field is also relevant. Although college training does not appear to differentiate between high and low performers, the college-trained individuals have shown greater flexibility and potential to move into higher levels within the organization.

A surprising number of low-producing individuals were recognized prior to their hiring as falling below Puritan-Bennett standards. In most cases, the hiring decision was made on a stereotyped notion that a particular type of individual might be better suited to a particular market. It is recommended that selection criteria not be altered significantly in the future.

Most high-producing sales individuals rate high on personal relations, training, and service-oriented skills, but low on skills showing assertiveness in power relationships such as working with dealers. With the shift away from hospital-based selling into dealer sales, the following should be considered: (1) to provide greater training related to dealer management and (2) to experiment selecting more assertive individuals, provided they show other desired talents.

The role of the sales manager is important in shaping the performance of both productive as well as less productive salesmen. Many case examples show individuals profiting from experience and development from their managers. Once again, the openness and receptivity to supervision on the part of the salesman seems critical.

In 1980, Owen Pinkerman decided to retire. He and John Francis were to select his replacement. I don't remember if a search organization was involved, but I was told that I would be interviewing three candidates, two from Hewlett-Packard and one from Sprint. I interviewed the person from Sprint, a senior staff member who seemed well versed in technology and marketing. From a psychological perspective, I considered him a viable candidate.

I was told that my next candidate would be from Hewlett-Packard. I was informed subsequently that the candidate refused to be assessed and that he was hired without an assessment. His name was Burton A. Dole Jr. I never met him. The first day of his employment, I was informed that I no longer was consulting with Puritan-Bennett. Both John Francis and Owen Pinkerman called to personally express their shock.

I never followed up with anyone. Pinkerman, who also left when Burton Dole started, called me a few times. During the 1980s, Puritan-Bennett fell behind industry leaders, with sales and profits falling significantly. Revenue increased only 4 percent between 1981 and 1984, and the company lost money in 1982 and 1984. With the introduction of the 7200 microprocessor ventilator, a new iteration of a standard Puritan-Bennett product, revenue increased as the 7200 became the most widely used ventilator in the world, with 60 percent market share by 1990.

John Francis retired in 1986, and Dole became the president, CEO, and chairman. The company's stock was in decline during the 1990s with stockholders urging a sale. Nellor acquired the company in 1995, changing the name to Nellor Puritan Bennett. Mallinckrodt bought Nellor in 1997.

Ironically, the selection of a new CEO was handled directly by Owen Pinkerman. Had Puritan followed a routine procedure of going through HR, Dole would have had his psychological assessment prior to his meeting with Francis and Pinkerman.

E. Y. Lingle, Seitz Packing Company

When I first started working with Harvey Thomas, he helped me call on some prospective clients in Kansas City. He also suggested that I should call on prospects in St. Joseph, Missouri, an industrial city with a population of 75,000 about 75 miles north of Kansas City. Thomas gave me the name of the general manager of Whitaker Cable, a former client that manufactured mileage cable for the automobile industry (a struggling company).

The person was very friendly and helpful, giving me the names of several people to contact. Cold calling, or sales of any kind, was new to me and not very comfortable. I can't remember my early calls, but I do remember coming back to visit my new friend at Whitaker Cable. When I came back for a third time, he greeted me with, "Get out of here! There's no business here!" I still remember the day vividly. It was probably the most poignant advice I ever received. In a flash, I realized that my future success was totally my responsibility.

It was the same afternoon that I had the good fortune to call on E. Y. Lingle, who with his lifelong friend and partner, Garland Wilson, both in their fifties, bought the Seitz Packing Company from the estate of Alfred J. Seitz in 1950. At the time, St. Joseph was a major packing-house center with a central stockyard. Seitz was a specialty company serving the sausage market (hot dogs and lunch meat) and an exclusive provider of prime steaks to high-end restaurants in New York City.

Lingle and Wilson were an excellent match. Lingle was a management and sales whiz and Wilson was an engineering and production whiz, and neither was interested in infringing on the other's domain. Alfred Seitz had been ill prior to his death, and the company had been under-capitalized and on the brink of failure. Lingle established the business plan, concentrated on a major advertising strategy for the Kansas City sausage market, and established the New York market for prime steaks. Wilson modernized and automated the production area and oversaw the construction of a new kill plant. The company was hugely success-ful.

Lingle and I bonded immediately. He was fascinated that a manage-ment psychologist walked into his office. He was interested in learning about me and my background. He brought Wilson in to meet me and had me explain what I did. I was impressed that Wilson accepted me right away, simply because Lingle accepted me. They both agreed to use me as a consultant, starting a long-term relationship. Lingle even had me assess his daughter, home from college, as a Christmas present.

I systematically provided assessments and feedback for their key staff members and learned about the company. Their products were the lead-ing sellers in the Kansas City market, and they took pride in produc-ing quality products. Wilson explained to me that their hot dogs were probably more nutritious than their prime steaks because the meat for hot dogs came from older animals with less fat.

During my career, I experienced three awesome sights in companies in which I consulted. One was my visit to the foundry at the Fairbanks Morse plant in Kansas City, Kansas, in which the smoke and fire seemed like hell on earth. Another was my first trip into an underground coal mine in Birmingham, Alabama, where the dust, darkness, cramped quarters, and live electrical lines seemed overwhelming. The third was my trip to the kill floor at the Seitz beef kill plant. The killed cattle hanging by their hind legs on a conveyor belt with blood spurting out from their throats is a scene not easily forgotten.

Seitz was not a large enough company to support much consulting time, but I made two or three visits a year for several years, until Lingle died unexpectedly. Wilson also retired. Lingle's son-in-law, Doug Esson, assumed Lingle's ownership. Wilson's son, who was working under his father, did not share the kind of relationship with Esson that Wilson shared with Lingle. In fact, it was so bad that Wilson, to his later regret, agreed to sell his share of ownership to Esson. The company continued to prosper, and Esson sold the company to Sara Lee in 1987.

Western Tablet and Stationery Company (Westab)

Another small client I acquired in St. Joseph through a cold call was the Western Tablet and Stationery Company (Westab), a company with a fascinating history. William Albrecht, the creator of the Big Chief writing tablet, opened Westab in St. Joseph in 1906. Practically every student in America during the first half of the nineteenth century bought Big Chief tablets. Westab became the world's largest paper company, with an imposing four-story office building with massive first floor windows resembling trendy Wall Street buildings of the era.

In 1920, the headquarters moved to Dayton, Ohio, but most manufacturing remained in St. Joseph. In Dayton, the company forged a unique relationship with the Mead Corporation. By the 1960s, the Big Chief line peaked, but Westab came up with another blockbuster invention—the spiral notebook.

By the time I called on Westab, St. Joseph was a regional office still manufacturing older products, but not new products like the spiral notebook. Walking in the front door of the Westab office was like walking back in time. The lobby was surrounded by a few massive, intimidating offices with large windows and old-fashioned shades. I asked for the president and was told he wasn't available, but I was greeted by Ron Smith, a man looking to be in his mid-forties, about five feet, seven inches tall and 140 pounds. He was wearing a tie and a white shirt with rolled-up sleeves, and I thought he was the office manager. It turned out that he was the general manager. The president, a relative of the founder, had a lifetime sinecure; he was president in name only.

Smith was a friendly, unpretentious person who listened carefully to what I said and who seemed to understand what I was saying without needing clarification. He said he had worked with psychologists in the past and found them to be helpful. He had been in his position for about a year. He was hired by the corporate group to put structure into the St. Joseph office in preparation for a complete takeover by Mead. Having once been the headquarters of the largest paper company in the world, the company had numerous bloodlines that never fully accepted the displacement to Dayton. St. Joseph was viewed more as a second headquarters rather than as a division with a diminishing manufacturing franchise. The relationship with Mead was further complicated by long-term agreements with family members that Mead was in the process of resolving.

As I became more familiar with the company, I came to recognize that not only did its buildings resemble an early nineteenth-century company, but it still retained an organizational structure out of step with modern management. For example, most of their salesmen had been with the company most of their work lives with large, mostly unmanageable territories in which they received commissions on everything sold, in their territories. In short, they were earning extremely high salaries capitalizing on the monopolistic sales of Big Chief tablets in territories lacking resources for developing new products and customers.

I walked in cold and within an hour had a new client I knew I would respect. Smith said he was interested primarily in the development of his future managers, and we worked up a schedule to assess him and his top staff. Over the next several months, I completed assessments on seven or eight people.

Smith didn't discuss the implications of an impending takeover by Mead, but I assumed that a massive reorganization was being discussed in Dayton. In addition to discussing my assessments with Smith, he used me as a sounding board to discuss his frustration with the Westab structure, the Westab modus operandi, and some of his expectations for the future of the company. I was anticipating an interesting and diverse relationship working with a knowledgeable, supportive client.

In the summer, I knew Smith would be on vacation. I received a telephone call from his secretary. While driving to California, Smith was killed in an auto accident.

One of the subordinates assumed his position on an acting basis. I continued my consulting for a few months to complete my commitments to provide feedback to individuals I had assessed. I discussed my status over the telephone with someone at the corporate office and was told that there would be a hold on my activity. Shortly thereafter, Westab was acquired formally by Mead, and I heard no more.

From its inception, Westab was a great corporate citizen to the city of St. Joseph. Westab engineers designed a 100-foot creation of Santa and his reindeer that sat atop the Westab headquarters roof each Christmas. With the acquisition of Westab, Mead continued the Christmas display up to 2001, when it sold the company and closed the plant. Today the city of St. Joseph shows the Westab Christmas display in one of the parks in the city.

Bret Armatas, Alvarado Manufacturing Company, Inc.

Alvarado Manufacturing Company in Chino, California, manufactures and sells pedestrian entry and exit control systems, such as manual turnstiles, optical turnstiles, gates and full-height turnstiles, posts, railings, and asset protection equipment, in three divisions servicing the business community, sports and entertainment venues, and retail store and warehouse facilities.

Alvarado was started in 1956 by Bill Alvarado, a fireman who made access control equipment, such as posts, railings, gates, and turnstiles for supermarkets and drugstores, in his garage. Theft, referred to as shrinkage, was a serious problem addressed by controlling access through cash register lines as the only way to exit. Alvarado sold his products through national sales representatives already selling shopping carts to supermarkets and drugstores.

As the business grew, the enterprise moved into a manufacturing facility in South El Monte, California. Alvarado's stepson, Victor (Vic) Robelet, worked in the business and assumed ownership at Alvarado's death. Alvarado evolved essentially as a job shop focused on expediting individual orders. As a unique request was completed, a new product was created, and Alvarado increased its product line to other grocery hardware items such as case and fixture protectors and full-height turnstiles. The full-height turnstiles also opened new industrial and recreational markets.

In 1980, a group of investors from the Kansas City area purchased the company, retaining Victor Robelet as national sales manager. The investors hired me to evaluate the management of the company and to assist in finding a company president. Joe Rutz, an engineer from the aerospace industry, was hired as president. I decided to purchase a minority interest in the company, eventually becoming the largest of approximately ten minority stockholders. In 1981, when an opportunity arose, I bought out the majority owner and all minority stockholders. I made an agreement with Rutz to run the company, with me essentially treating the company as an investment and my financial statement providing working capital.

Running the company was a difficult job. A job shop mentality requires hands-on expertise with minimal regard for systems and controls. The workforce of approximately seventy people was indispensable due to their loyalty and experience; however, they lacked education and experience to operate in a formal structure.

With new management came a realization that future growth and even survival were dependent on making the transition from job shop to a fully integrated manufacturing operation. Specifically, we also strived for organic growth through the development and introduction of technology into the product line. A major accomplishment was the development of a new, streamlined three-armed turnstile to compete in sports stadiums and industrial markets in which the three-armed turnstile with resettable and non-resettable counters was standard. Over eight years, annual sales tripled.

The company's main administrative and manufacturing facility is in Chino, California, just east of Los Angeles on the 60 freeway and seven miles from the Ontario airport, in a 70,000-square-foot building. The building is owned by the Armatas Family Trust. From my consulting experience, I learned about diversifying my investments.

I hired a replacement for Joe Rutz as general manager in 1989. During the replacement's tenure, the company sought to grow and expand. Graduate design engineers and sales staff were added, including the promotion of Bill Voss from inside sales to western regional sales manager. Competent staff were hired in production, including Jim Mitroff as production manager. Much of the new general manager's time was spent seeking out acquisition candidates. Shortly after his hire, it became obvious that his strategy was inconsistent with Alvarado's financial condition, and the company began suffering significant losses. I terminated the general manager and most nonessential staff and services he added.

Back to the Basics

After the removal of the general manager in 1990, the company was left with a management group of Vic Robelet (in Chicago) and Mitroff and Voss at the home office. Although I was still working full-time in my consulting practice, I assumed the position of CEO of the company with a commitment from the staff to cut costs and return to the basics by concentrating on serving the customer base and by not taking on projects beyond our normal capability.

Ironically, at this time, Burle Industries, a surveillance camera company that had recently been spun off from Radio Corporation of America (RCA) made an unsolicited bid to purchase Alvarado. The cash offer for the stock of the company and repayment of company loans was well beyond my expectation, but I turned down the offer, preferring to keep Alvarado as a personal investment.

Within the existing management group, Jim Mitroff emerged as the strongest leader, and he soon became general manager. The workforce was largely nonprofessional and Jim Mitroff's dominant management style proved to be successful in pursuing the specific, basic objectives sought by the company. Within a few months, the company became profitable.

For five straight years, the company showed continued growth and profitability with sales doubling. The next three years were profitable, but sales flattened, primarily due to a significant drop in retail sales. The introduction of an open design in supermarkets and drugstores eliminated the need for posts, railings, and turnstiles.

A Move to Technology

In the latter part of 1995, I embarked on a strategic plan designed to make Alvarado a more technology-driven company. My son, Bret Armatas, formerly a trial lawyer, joined the company as vice president of sales and marketing. Based in Kansas City, one of his responsibilities was to spearhead technology sales. A separate software function was formed in 1996 by me to develop software programs complementary to Alvarado turnstile hardware. A significant hire was Chris Bednarski, an established software engineer who is still employed at Alvarado. The engineering group subsequently added an electrical engineer and a product/project engineer.

A breakthrough arose in a project with the Cleveland Indians to provide the new Jacobs Field with access-controlled modules consisting of forty-two Alvarado turnstiles combined with proprietary GateLink and GateWatch software, providing ticket access, patron/vehicle counting, and point-of-sale coordination. A new vista opened for servicing sports and entertainment venues. What followed quickly were major projects with all Six Flags theme parks, Universal's Islands of Adventure, and all of Holland America's ships. These were the start of what made Alvarado one of the nation's leaders in providing integrated access control systems.

The focus of integrated systems requires a different sales mentality than that of selling hardware. Most of the projects require significant background work, formal proposals, and project management. Bret Armatas's organizational and literary skills had a major impact on providing meaningful focus, sales materials, user manuals, and professional proposals.

While sales increased consistently in industrial security and entertainment, operations had difficulty adjusting to the increased demands of a more diversified product mix. In 1997, I took a more active role in the company. Victor Robelet was brought back as retail sales manager with a company commitment to provide the retail market with new products. Market centers were established with Robelet responsible for retail, Voss responsible for security, and Bret Armatas responsible for entertainment.

The reorganization resulted in new retail market products, including a gravity gate enclosure, a new floor bumper case protector, and the Watchman 2000. The gravity gate and the case protector both became standard features, building sales and customer satisfaction. The Watchman 2000, a patented warning device that warns forklift or Towmotor operators of impending collisions with automatic doors and other overhead fixtures, became a leader in warehouse sales.

In the industrial security area, Alvarado introduced optical counting lanes and optical access control lanes that offered new high-end aesthetic products to corporate and public venues. As world safety concerns grew in time, Alvarado's optical access control products became sales leaders for the company.

Access control hardware is almost always used as part of an overall system. For a hardware-only manufacturer, like Alvarado prior to developing proprietary software products, this inevitably meant that someone else, whether a dealer, an integrator, or the like, managed the project.

Alvarado's focus in the leisure and entertainment and security markets was to provide comprehensive solutions within its sphere of expertise and to increase the solutions it could provide as its sphere of expertise increased. This was the impetus for developing software capability and for creating national and international sales territories staffed by a company-trained sales staff.

Jorgen Burch joined the company as an interim vice president of operations on April 1, 1998. Burch had a strong background in production and general management in Denmark. At Alvarado, key positions were filled in materials management, production management, and sales engineering. The company refocused the order/material/production flow in working toward making operational a $200,000-plus computer system.

By operating out of Kansas City, Bret Armatas was cut off from meaningful communication with the corporate group and considered leaving the company. After evaluating options, he accepted the position of president and moved to California. Without a background in manufacturing, Bret Armatas had a learning curve in a complex environment. Jack Horner, a former manufacturing manager at Alvarado who subsequently had worked as a sales agent, returned to Alvarado as operations manager.

Horner was a great addition, holding the plant together as Bret Armatas assimilated knowledge of the company. A significant personal development move involved Bret Armatas joining a management development group with other executives sponsored by Michael Milken, which provided ongoing feedback as he confronted new issues. Other significant moves included hiring an older, experienced controller and an experienced purchasing manager.

Although I held the title of CEO, Bret Armatas had operational autonomy as president. A major undertaking was in a systematic approach to build a qualified, experienced staff. New hires often brought new knowledge, ideas, experience, and the capability to advance systems and technology.

Another major undertaking was in establishing manufacturing networks primarily in China but also in India. A significant contribution was made by an American management consultant with roots in China who made repeated trips overseas with Bret Armatas to line up multiple contractors to provide hardware and parts that were assembled at the Alvarado manufacturing plant.

Although Alvarado had competent electrical and mechanical engineers, they didn't have design engineers. Bret Armatas made a significant decision in outsourcing the design of new optical lanes and speed gates, leading to Alvarado's success as a leader in the pedestrian entry control market. Years later, when I read a biography on Steve Jobs, I realized that part of his genius was in always using designers and never allowing engineers to design new products.

Alvarado was organized into three product divisions: security entry control, sports and entertainment, and asset protection and crowd control.

Its core competencies focus on the following:

1. Customer centric—from its inception as a job shop, Alvarado has grown by adding products that customers need
2. Continuous operational improvement
3. Strong network of integrators, dealers, and loyal partners

After 9/11 and a continuous rise in terrorist activities seen globally, pedestrian entry control, consisting of aesthetically engineered optical lanes and speed gates, provided the greatest increase in sales and revenue. In the construction of office entrances or new office buildings, entrance security is a major consideration.

In a 2017 analysis of global access control companies, Alvarado was acknowledged as the second largest company in America and the sixth largest in the world. Alvarado was the number one seller of pedestrian entry control systems in America.

The transition from a job shop to the efficient technology company it is today was an arduous task. Joe Rutz set the mission of pointing the company toward technology in introducing the three-armed turnstile. The next great move was the introduction of software and the breakthrough contract with the Cleveland Indians. Finally, the evolving leadership of Bret Armatas kept the momentum on track.

Almost forty years of family ownership demonstrates the rewards that can occur by setting growth goals while maintaining conservative financial controls. Two financial crises were weathered. The first, after an ambitious expansion, was resolved by a move back to the basics. Costs were cut, personnel were eliminated, and an expansion-by-acquisition strategy was eliminated. The second was the elimination of shrinkage controls by supermarkets and drugstores that significantly reduced the company's largest market. A conservative approach to financing enabled the company to weather a crisis while other markets matured.

On June 27, 2019, while preparing this memoir for publication, it was announced that the Alvarado Manufacturing Company was acquired in a cash transaction by Dormakaba Holding AG of Rümlang, Switzerland, a global leader in the manufacturing of access control and security solutions with over $2 billion in annual sales. Bret Armatas agreed to a two-year contract to oversee the transaction.

In reflecting about the Alvarado success, I come back to the lessons from Jack Welch at GE and Harold Geneen at ITT: Hire the best and the brightest, but recognize and provide for continuous education and broadening of experience.

Comments

Puritan-Bennett was a major client. It was an oligopoly founded by a domineering entrepreneur. Puritan-Bennett had an interesting family history and a unique organizational structure.

E. Y. Lingle was the marketing partner in Seitz Packing Company with the ingenuity to create quasi-monopolistic markets for mundane products. The creation of a compatible partnership ensured quality-controlled production as a barrier for competition.

Western Tablet and Stationery Company was a history lesson, as I consulted with a company that at one time was the largest paper company in the world and the monopolistic owner of two blockbuster trademarks. With such a monopoly, a company can create and perpetuate undesirable practices, ultimately leading to its demise. Westab's insider activities were so intrusive, a clear contract of sale could not be finalized for years.

For almost twenty-five years, I was the sole owner of Alvarado Manufacturing Company. Then I turned over my majority interest to my son, Bret. The goal of adding technology to the product line and system to the organization was an ambitious task finalized by Bret Armatas.

Peter Drucker cautioned that entrepreneurial companies need long-term perspectives to ensure survival. Alvarado survived two financial crises but eventually emerged with its own quasi-monopoly in pedestrian entry control systems. The company, as a leader in the industry, was sold at a premium valuation.

CHAPTER EIGHT

FINAL COMMENTS

I n the years following World War II, many great American companies enjoyed monopolistic advantages in such areas as product development, captive markets, technology, and experienced workforces. It was during this era that my consulting practice evolved. My client base included ITT and Colt Industries, two of the most successful and best-managed conglomerates in the world, and an assortment of highly successful, closely controlled public and private companies.

As the competition from both American and international companies advanced, the monopolies diminished, revealing the bloating and expense of their production, leading to the great American recession.

For many years, most large American companies showed unusual stability and resistance to change. A job with IBM, General Motors, or a public utility led to a career path culminating eventually in a secure pension.

The turmoil of the 1980s and 1990s has changed that pattern. Downsized companies keep management structures flat by eliminating mid-level management jobs. In 1987, one in twenty workers were in management. Today's students are facing a trend leading to one in fifty workers in management.

During the downturn, most conglomerates, including ITT and Colt Industries, were replaced by newer concepts such as focusing on a single company's core competencies. Both ITT and Colt Industries were sold off with substantial gains for the executives and stockholders. Although the two companies no longer exist, their management controls and systems serve as guidelines and a model today for the management of multidivisional companies.

The changing structure of American business has been taking place concurrently with a great social revolution toward greater democratization in American and international institutions. An ironic paradox exists in which workers today feel they have entitlement to greater job and management involvement at a time when management opportunities are limited.

We have seen profound effects from the paradoxical changes in American industry. An increasing group of disappointed, frustrated, displaced executives are unemployed or serving in non-management lower-paid jobs. Conversely, we have seen American industry become stronger and more competitive as managers demonstrate resourcefulness and as management rewards become more clearly based on performance.

America has also seen a proliferation of start-up organizations. The technical revolution has been the genesis for an ever-expanding new breed of entrepreneurs. Even with established organizations, more openings are available to highly competitive, entrepreneurial-type individuals.

The Internet alone has spurred a plethora of new, independent entrepreneurs in enterprises not even dreamed of a generation ago. One of the clients highlighted in this memoir is James (Jim) O'Crowley, the unique founder of Coalter Investment, a one-person enterprise. There is nothing unique about the thousands of one-person enterprises in America today.

As American management changes, our understanding of entrepreneurs also changes. A little more than a generation ago, the term *entrepreneur* seemed to be interchangeable with such terms as start-up, unorganized, freewheeling, or out of control. The entrepreneurial organization at that time was characterized as an organization that had a product and sales niche that had limited growth, depending on the complexity of the product, the manufacturing processes, or the markets. Increased sales required a focus on planning—infrastructure development and organization—with the logical assumption that the personality of the entrepreneur must be subdued and/or his or her power decentralized.

Outdated generalizations about entrepreneurs are no longer valid. Many CEOs in gigantic organizations provide an entrepreneurial structure and a creative environment for their employees without giving up their centralized power or their accountability for setting the course and direction of the company.

The key, of course, lies in the fact that the CEO has the power to shape the organization. Smart CEOs keep the organization simple and basic with a minimum of hierarchy and bureaucracy. They don't lose their entrepreneurial perspective. They are willing to change and experiment.

My Memoir

In my effort to memorialize the executives with whom I consulted during my career, I realized that I had described models depicting the structure and strategies of successful, multidivisional companies and successful independent enterprises.

In a classic paper written two generations ago, Peter Drucker outlined the five critical steps for the survival of an entrepreneurial enterprise.[15] Most of my clients or their spin-offs are still in business, available as models for today's CEOs and aspiring entrepreneurs.

I started my memoir with the purpose of describing three recently deceased successful executives and their companies with whom I had long-term consulting relationships. Belatedly, I decided to also include in my memoir more than twenty-five leaders and companies with whom I consulted over my fifty-year consulting practice. Included are executives and companies with both long-term and short-term relationships. All companies were successful and enlightened—and willing to spend consulting dollars on the personal development of existing and promising future executives.

In organizing the memoir, I assigned clients to homogeneous groups including my top three entrepreneurial executives, conglomerates, multidivisional companies, legal monopolies, service companies, restaurants, and manufacturers. I also recognized that most of the leaders in my client companies had unique management skills, styles, and practices. There is something meaningful to be learned from each of the companies and the management style and practices of each of their leaders.

In terms of priority, my concentration is centered on the three individually focused companies and their entrepreneurial CEOs and two conglomerates and their significant contributors. The individual company executives are Del Dunmire and Growth Industries, Garry Drummond and the Drummond Company, Inc., and Dave Noble and American Equity Investment Life Insurance Company. The conglomerate companies are ITT with Harold Geneen and Colt Industries, Inc. with George Strichman, their respective CEOs.

I selected the two groups because of my long-standing relationships with each of the companies and the relevance of the companies today as models for executives.

The three CEOs and their similar management styles are described in chapter one, "Three Entrepreneurs":

> They were dominating leaders, clearly in control of their companies and committed totally to their companies. They had a clear picture of areas of accountability and were quick to identify problems. Bureaucracies were stifled by open communication. Unexpected surprises were minimized. Each sought to capitalize on technology in their products or services. Each tried to create quality products, services, and relationships that could result in monopolistic or quasi-monopolistic relationships or prices enhanced by strategic sales efforts. They thoroughly understood their markets and established close personal relationships with their customers. They all valued the contributions of outside consultants and were open to change.

The conglomerates are described in chapter two, "Conglomerates: ITT Corporation and Colt Industries":

> Although most conglomerates are gone, what is not gone is the amazing system of management control exercised by ITT and Colt Industries. The systems worked for conglomerates. They are just as effective applied to the massive multidivisional companies operating globally today.

The multidivisional model depicted by ITT and Colt Industries was focused on selecting the best and the brightest through a system of psychological assessments coordinated by an internal psychology staff; however, the real strength of the model was in the following:

- The tight central control with substantial, competent headquarters staff
- Experienced group vice presidents
- Matrix management checks and balances
- Clear, measured MBO accountabilities
- Staff line production managers
- A corporate psychology function as part of HR

The theme of these successful companies is strong central control and the establishment of accountabilities. Del Dunmire expounds on the virtue of his basic company that both survives and profits in downturns. Harold Geneen expounds on his no-surprises approach to management. Consider that 99 percent of surprises in business are negative; any CEO who can reduce surprises can outperform competitors.

Of the CEOs described in the multidivisional chapter, Harold Hook stands out with his own system of central control. His accomplishments at American General are impressive.

Although I list manufacturing companies in the last chapter, two-thirds of my time was spent consulting with manufacturing and mining companies. In addition to the companies listed in the manufacturing section are Growth Industries, the Drummond Company, and six separate Colt Industries manufacturing plants.

As I explain throughout this memoir, for many reasons, companies that seem to be successful are hesitant to seek change, thus minimizing the potential contribution of a psychologist with an organizational development background. As I mention in the manufacturing chapter, there are so many moving parts in a manufacturing company that problems, needing solutions, are routine. Thus, manufacturing companies are more open to change and more active in seeking change.

My experience with legal monopolies was limited, but the vignettes in the chapter are fascinating. Bureaucratic factors become institutionalized, but monopolies do not last forever.

The service chapter has some outstanding models to follow. BMA was an exemplary large enterprise company with outstanding leaders, a talented professional staff, and a reputation as a sterling corporate citizen. They sold the insurance holdings at a propitious time. Entrepreneurs Walter W. Ross (Beta Sigma Phi) and James (Jim) Barickman (Barickman Advertising) built impressive growth companies.

The restaurant chapter is devoted to Richard (Rick) Harman and the outstanding history of the restaurant industry in Kansas City, Missouri.

Early in this memoir, I wrote that Harvey Thomas, my first mentor, told me that I would learn from my clients. Now I realize that many of my past experiences were naive at the time in the sense that I had not yet learned what I needed to know. As time has passed, I've learned much about what it takes to be a successful CEO. I've learned that monopolies end, that bureaucracies block progress, and that change starts at the top.

I've also learned that successful companies can be modeled. For that reason, I decided to highlight the management examples of Messrs. Dunmire, Drummond, Noble, Geneen, and Strichman.

I've also analyzed initial psychological assessments and behavior patterns of the executives and entrepreneurs discussed in this memoir. The CEOs whom I interviewed, without exception, were seen by themselves and others as being intelligent, conceptual, competitive, management-type individuals. More significantly, they also generally demonstrate flexible, adaptable personalities indicating social versatility in responding to diverse interpersonal situations. None could be labeled as consistently showing extreme behaviors such as narcissism or autocracy. Even Harold Geneen had been described as a regular person when he was not conducting his no-surprises management sessions.

It appears that the role of executive is seen universally to require the services of what Harold Geneen saw as the best and the brightest: a self-sufficient, competitive but adaptable person who has prepared for a management career and demonstrated tangible accomplishments. People who succeed seem to understand their roles, and people who hire them seem to be looking for just such individuals. A significant part of my practice was in assisting in identifying such individuals. A significant part of my feedback sessions involved assisting individuals in exploring their past management progression and strategies for the future.

Once the best and brightest presidential candidates were selected, both ITT and Colt Industries sought relevant experience in a president, followed by a system of accountability supplemented by continuous feedback from a higher authority (e.g., ITT's Harold Geneen himself or Colt's technically proficient group vice presidents). Harold Hook developed a standardized educational system to make sure that all executives were always on the same page.

A major organizational issue involves centralized versus decentralized management structures. Without exception, the most effective companies with which I consulted had strong central controls vested primarily with the CEO. Self-directed, self-actualizing theories were treated as just that—theories! These companies were willing to forgo the loss of an outstanding prospect unwilling to fit into the established system.

The first chapter of Harold Geneen's book *Managing* begins with the following:

Theory G: You cannot run a business, or anything else, on a theory.

What Geneen goes on to explain is that a company, its chief executive, and the entire management team are judged by one criterion—long-term performance. I could add: a "best and brightest" executive with enlightened HR and with consulting psychological resources can play an important role in achieving such an objective.

Postscript

During my long career, I had the dual experience of both consulting to CEOs and being a CEO in my own successful manufacturing company. There is a pejorative idiom attributed to George Bernard Shaw: "Those who can, do; those who can't, teach." I can honestly say that I have been able to practice what I preach!

HISTORY OF
ORGANIZATIONAL MANAGEMENT

Scientific Management

Management as a discipline evolved from the complexities encountered in producing goods and equipment during the Industrial Revolution. The scientific management movement at the start of the twentieth century, credited largely to the efforts of Frederick W. Taylor and Frank Gilbreth, had the greatest impact on modern management practices. Both men were concerned with improving the efficiency and technology of industry by conducting numerous experiments to create worker efficiency and to reduce human exertion. Their efforts led to revolutionary practices, introduced as human engineering, that are related to systems, work simplification, standardization, communication, and management control.

As Taylor, in his 1911 book, *The Principles of Scientific Management*, declared,

> The idea is of . . . training a workman under a competent teacher into new working habits until he continually and habitually works in accordance with scientific laws, which

have been developed by someone else, is directly antagonistic to the old idea that each workman can best regulate his own way of doing his work . . . The philosophy of the old management puts the entire responsibility upon the workmen, while the philosophy of the new places a great part of it upon the management.[16]

Perhaps the greatest impact on the scientific management movement was in transforming marginally subsisting laborers into semiskilled workers of today's mass production industries with attendant middle-class standards of living and income security. To direct and control these workers, management evolved as a discipline with independent culture and technology.

Among the criticism of scientific management is the mechanical practice of programming the jobs of workers, much as machines are programmed. Scientific management established an authoritarian management model that prevailed through the Great Depression and into World War II. As labor became more automated, fewer laborers were needed. As companies grew and established bureaucracies and monopolistic advantages in their markets, more management positions were created, often leading to layering of managers performing the same function.

Line and Staff: The Military Management Model

Throughout history, successful leaders have demonstrated the ability to create and manage large, powerful, and disciplined military forces. The names of Alexander the Great, Julius Caesar, and Napoleon quickly come to mind, but great militaries historically have learned from others and for generations have followed a line-and-staff organizational structure. A line organization engages in battle. The staff organization provides support to the line. Everyone clearly knows, understands, and accepts the authority accorded to each rank in the system.

With knowledge of such a time-honored system, larger centralized corporations have also adhered to a line-and-staff organizational structure for generations. In the corporate world, line-and-staff management has two separate hierarchies:

1. The line hierarchy in which the departments are revenue generators (manufacturing, selling) and their managers are responsible for achieving the organization's main objectives by executing the key functions (such as policy making, target setting, and decision-making)

2. The staff hierarchy, in which the departments are revenue consumers, and their managers are responsible for activities that support line functions (such as accounting, maintenance, and HR)

While both hierarchies have their own chains of command, a line manager may have direct control over staff employees, but a staff manager may have no such power over the line employees. In modern practice, the difference in the two hierarchies is not so clear-cut, and jobs often have elements of both types of functions.

Manufacturing companies typically have three major line functions comprised of an engineering/design group, a manufacturing group, and a sales/marketing group. Colt Industries had independent "staff-line" managers to assist in the coordination of these major line functions.

The Human Relations Movement

Elton Mayo

Elton Mayo was an Australian-born psychologist, industrial researcher, and organizational theorist who was appointed to Harvard Business School in 1926 as a professor of industrial research.[17] His work helped to lay the foundation for the human relations movement.

Mayo's major project, known as the Hawthorne studies, took place at the Western Electric Hawthorne plant in Cicero, Illinois. His team carried out experiments for improving productivity, involving manipulating length of rest and lunch periods and piecework payment plans. Mayo concluded that work performance is dependent on both social relationships and job content. He suggested a tension between workers' *logic of sentiment* and managers' *logic of cost and efficiency* that could lead to conflict within organizations. Workers responded to management pressure simply by restricting production to levels they felt were appropriate.

During the Depression and World War II eras, several significant social psychologists, clinical psychologists, and philosophers were addressing human relations management issues derived from personality theories.

Carl Rogers

Carl Rogers, a clinical psychologist whose client-centered psychotherapy relied firmly on the growth motivation of the client to resolve his or her problems, had a significant impact on a field dominated by Freudians.[18] The Rogerian nondirective therapist communicates his nonjudgmental empathy and understanding of the client as he or she struggles with here-and-now issues.

Central to Rogerian theory is the notion of *self-concept*, an internalized frame of reference that guides behavior and stresses the uniqueness and individual differences among people. A competent leader should be sensitive and responsive to these individual differences.

Nondirective concepts have been adapted universally into methodologies for counseling clients in multiple disciplines, including business and management in general and specifically in human resource areas. As a graduate student in a personnel management curriculum at the University of Colorado, my favorite course was a nondirective practicum taught by a professor who studied under Carl Rogers at Ohio State University.

Abraham Maslow

Abraham Maslow was a humanistic psychologist in the 1940s–1960s who also spearheaded a movement that emphasized the positive potential of human beings.[19] He believed that all people have a strong desire to realize their full potential—to reach a level of self-actualization. His studies concentrated on mentally healthy individuals representing optimal psychological health and functioning, including case studies on historical figures such as Albert Einstein and Henry David Thoreau. He discovered all had similar personality traits:

> Reality centered, able to differentiate what was fraudulent from what was genuine; problem centered, meaning that they treated life's difficulties as problems that demanded solutions; healthy personal relationships, but comfortable being alone; spontaneous and creative; not bound too strictly by social conventions.

Maslow defined self-actualization as achieving the fullest use of one's talents and interests—"the need to become everything one is capable of becoming." Self-actualization is highly individualistic and reflects the premise that the self is "sovereign and inviolable."

Maslow described human needs as ordered in a prepotent hierarchy of drives—a pressing lower need would need to be mostly satisfied before someone would be driven to the next higher need. The physiological need was the lowest. The advanced levels included safety, love/belonging, esteem, and, ultimately, self-actualization.

Frederick Herzberg

Frederick Herzberg, a professor of management at Case Western Reserve University, elaborated on Maslow's personality theories with the proposed motivator-hygiene theory, also known as the two-factor theory of job satisfaction.[20] His theory was a direct application of relating human drives to work applications. According to his theory, people are influenced by two sets of factors:

1. Hygiene factors will not motivate, but if they are missing, they can lower motivation. Hygiene factors can be such things as physical surroundings, a reasonable level of pay, and job security. The theory deals with satisfaction and dissatisfaction in jobs that are not affected by the same sets of needs but occur independently of each other.

2. Motivational factors will not necessarily lower motivation, but they can be responsible for increasing motivation. Motivational factors, referred to as growth factors, include such things as achievement, challenge, job recognition, potential for advancement, self-determination, and the job itself.

Douglas McGregor

Douglas McGregor is known as the creator and developer of the famous Theory X and Theory Y theories of human motivation and management.[21] Developed during the 1960s, the theories describe contrast-
ing models of workforce motivation. According to the models, the two
opposing sets of general assumptions of how workers are motivated
form the basis for two different managerial styles:

1. Theory X is based on pessimistic assumptions regarding the typical worker, assuming the typical worker has little ambition and
   shies away from work or responsibilities. Theory X–style managers believe their workers are less intelligent, lazy, and work solely
   for a sustainable income. McGregor describes two approaches to
   implementing Theory X, a *hard*, intimidating approach with an
   imminent use of punishment, and a *soft*, less-regulated approach
   designed to win over cooperation. McGregor feels that effective
   Theory X managers use a combination of both approaches and
   that with their tight control, Theory X managers show the greatest
   consistency in performance.
2. Theory Y managers believe people in the workforce are internally
   motivated and work to improve themselves without needing a direct reward in return. Theory Y employees are regarded as valuable
   assets of the company who tend to take full responsibility for their
   work and who respond best to a democratic style of leadership.

Although McGregor's theories are close to those of Maslow and clearly
show his personal preference for a Theory Y model, he recognizes that
a combination of both theories may be appropriate. Theory Y leaves
room for error in terms of consistency and uniformity.

The common thread of the management approaches described in this section is their creative philosophical origins. The post–World War II era with such dramatic changes in personal growth and opportunity demanded such activity in preparation for future growth in complex, technically driven management expansions. Concepts such as self-actualization were optimistic and encouraging both to students and management. Business school graduates knew what types of companies they were attracted to and companies knew who they were looking to recruit.

As exciting and popular as self-actualizing theories were, a caveat often missed was the fact that the practitioners were dealing with theories, not empirical facts. In my long consulting career, I encountered several outstanding companies that experienced disastrous results by failing to hold key managers accountable for their performance.

Social Psychology, Kurt Lewin

Kurt Lewin was a German-American psychologist, known as the father of social psychology, group dynamics, and organizational development.[22] Immigrating to America in 1933, he was a professor at Stanford, Cornell University, and the University of Iowa as well as director of the Center for Group Dynamics at MIT. Lewin distinguished himself as a prolific practical theorist and applied researcher.

A classic study during World War II attempted to determine the most effective way to educate American housewives in the preparation of animal parts that historically had been considered as undesirable. The methodology compared the teachings by an authoritarian lecturer, a laissez-faire lecturer, and a discussion leader. The results demonstrated the overwhelming effectiveness of group decision-making, the forerunner of group dynamics.

As an applied researcher, Lewin became a master at transposing an everyday problem into a psychological experiment. He minimized nature/nurture polemics with his interpretation of behavior being a function of a person operating in an environment, B=f(P,E). His interpretations of behavior led to a focus on phenomenological exploration of social systems and the analysis of helping forces toward a goal or hindering forces blocking movement toward a goal, what is known as Lewin's Field Theory.

Lewin first coined the term *action research* as a comparative social action research that uses a spiral of steps, each of which is composed of a circle of planning, action, and fact-finding about the result of the action. It is an applied research methodology that I have used throughout my professional life.

While at MIT, he was charged with finding an effective way to combat religious and racial prejudices and set up a workshop to conduct a change experiment for what is now known as sensitivity training. In 1947, this procedure led to the establishment of the National Training Laboratories (NTL) in Bethel, Maine. Carl Rogers believed that sensitivity training is "perhaps the most significant social invention of the century."

Lewin developed an early model of understanding dynamic change in groups as a three-stage process. The first stage he called *unfreezing*. It involved overcoming inertia and dismantling the existing mindset. In the second stage, change occurs in a period of confusion and transition. The third phase, he named *freezing*—crystallizing a new mindset.

In a 1947 article, Lewin coined the term *group dynamics*, defining a field regarding the nature of groups—their laws, establishment, development, and interactions with other groups, individuals, and institutions. With his background in Gestalt psychology, Lewin justified group existence using the dictum "The whole is greater than the sum of its parts." He theorized that when a group is established, it becomes a unified system with supervening qualities that cannot be understood by evaluating members individually. The study of group dynamics remains relevant today in which a vast number of professions (e.g., business and industry, industrial/management psychology, clinical/counseling psychology, and sports and recreation) rely on its mechanisms to thrive.

The National Training Laboratories, now known as the NTL Institute for Applied Behavioral Science, has had a significant impact in the direct and indirect development of managers as companies evolved from authoritarian scientific management roots. Today's managers operate in organizations in which courses in organizational development are standard in business schools and most HR functions provide internal organization development and consultation.

At the center of NTL's service since inception in 1947 has been the Training Laboratory (T-Group) in which executives learn group dynamics through experience, not lecture. The T-Group sessions are usually in one-week, intense peer-group training sessions in which stature, beliefs, and established behavior patterns are challenged.

The T-Group model was adopted quickly in graduate psychology and business management by major universities. From the early 1960s, I have been involved with T-Group programs, both as a participant and as a trainer. Although the concept was enthusiastically accepted by professional consultants, the changes in philosophy and practice learned by trainees were not necessarily transferable to their jobs.

I remember reading an extensive report in the *Wall Street Journal* in the early 1960s about a one-year follow-up study of key employees from major American corporations who participated in NTL T-Group sessions. Although some participants and their corporations reported glowing reports, many participants discovered resistance when trying to put into practice what they learned at NTL.

After all these years, I remembered the *Journal* article because it had an impact on me at the time, reinforcing something I learned when I started consulting to management. I discovered that companies hiring psychologists like me were successful companies looking to develop management skills in their executives; however, as successful companies, they were not seeking organizational change.

Organizational Development

In the late 1950s and early 1960s, expansion of management requirements, in addition to rapid organizational expansion, intensified the need for planned management succession and development programs. In addition, decentralization, the growth of computers, and geographic expansion required the development of effective information systems. In the mid-1960s, a new focus was on total system change. The organizational dilemma was to achieve the organization's mission while maintaining a growing organization of people with personal needs for worth, growth, and satisfaction.[23]

In the mid-1960s to 1970s, the primary providers of organizational direction to companies were a select group of consultants from major universities. These individuals in turn established close relationships, sharing information to define the question, what is organizational development? The answer was a seven-step definition defined as:

1. A planned change effort
2. Involving the total system
3. Managed from the top
4. Designed to increase organization effectiveness and health
5. Achieving its goals through planned interventions using behavioral science knowledge
6. Focuses on changing attitudes and/or behavior
7. Usually relies on some form of experienced-based learning

Although a consensus was achieved, each consultant had already published numerous philosophical and applied books and papers related to elements of organizational development. Through the Addison-Wesley Publishing Company, various consultants collaborated to write a series of six practical booklets of approximately 150 pages each, describing how they facilitated specific case studies including goals, strategies, workshops, interventions, tools, and materials used. Many workshops contained action research projects and specific interventions, such as Richard Beckhard's "confrontation meeting," which became a standard intervention used by organizational development leaders internationally.

From a theoretical and conceptual level, there is little doubt of the value and effectiveness of organizational development tools and interventions, particularly if managed from the top. From my personal experience, as I report in the vignette chapters, organizational development was still a work in progress. Executives at the top of successful companies did not typically set a high priority on seeking change.

Peter Drucker, Management by Objectives (MBO)

The books on formalized goal-setting systems are legion in number, but Peter Drucker and Douglas McGregor are generally credited with providing the foundation for management by objectives in use today. MBO is a management concept that has gained popularity since being introduced by Drucker in his 1954 writings:[24]

Management by objectives is a process by which work is organized in terms of achieving specific objectives within set time limits. Most authors agree that in the system of MBO, the superior and subordinate jointly

1. Specify, in writing, the major functional areas of responsibility for the subordinate, including goals to be accomplished in terms of results, and
2. Determine how and within what time frame the agreed-upon standards should be achieved, so that the superior and the subordinate can periodically evaluate progress.

If the conditions of MBO are satisfied, then the following expectations follow logically:

1. The decision-making and control processed within the company should show direct improvement, and
2. Employee satisfaction increases as a by-product.

Society for Industrial and Organizational Psychology

The American Psychological Association (APA) was founded in 1892 and dedicated to the field of experimental psychology. It was psychology's move to be identified as a true science, not unlike other sciences such as chemistry, physics, and biology. As such, it disavowed any relationship to applied psychology of any persuasion, such as clinical, counseling, educational, or industrial psychology. APA's decision notwithstanding, applied psychology practices grew dramatically and formed their own associations in 1921 and 1937. In 1945, all psychologists were merged into the American Psychological Association, with the experimental groups comprising only a few small divisions in an association today that has over 200,000 members in sixty divisions.

Initially, Division 14 of the APA was called the Industrial and Business Psychology Division. In 1982, to resolve "tension between science and practice," the APA Division 14 was incorporated as the Society for Industrial and Organizational Psychology (SIOP), gaining an independent and secure base. I have been a member of Division 14 in both iterations.

SIOP members follow a researcher/practitioner model and are responsible for most of the organizational development research, practice, and consultation undertaken with American industry. The requirement for membership in SIOP is a doctoral degree with a research thesis from a university psychological program approved by the American Psychological Association. Most SIOP members also hold memberships in other APA divisions, such as clinical, counseling, or educational.

SIOP also has associate members with required psychology master's degrees from APA-approved universities. Associates mainly work in HR areas as internal consultants in major corporations, overseeing organizational development workshops and research projects.

ABOUT THE AUTHOR

James P. Armatas has enjoyed a fifty-year career as a psychological consultant to a diverse group of successful CEO clients and their companies. With a background in clinical counseling and organizational psychology, Armatas has also held positions in the United States Department of Veterans Affairs as an instructor and visiting professor in the Department of Psychology at the University of Kansas, and as the owner and CEO of Alvarado Manufacturing Company, Inc.

NOTES

1 Peter F. Drucker, "Business Objectives and Survival Needs," in *Technology, Management and Society* (New York: Harper & Row, 1970).

2 Lee J. Cronbach, *Essentials of Psychological Testing* (New York: Harper & Row, 1949).

3 Gordon W. Allport, *The American Journal* (1937).

4 Paul E. Meehl, *Clinical vs. Statistical Prediction* (Minneapolis: University of Minnesota Press, 1954).

5 James P. Armatas, Hewitt, J.L., Lohrenz, L.J., *Rehabilitation of the Chronically Institutionalized*, Leavenworth Veterans Administration Center, 1970.

6 Harry Stack Sullivan, *The Interpersonal Theory of Psychiatry*, New York: Norton, 1953.

7 Harold Geneen and Alvin Moscow, *Managing* (New York: Doubleday & Company, 1984).

8 Geneen and Moscow, *Managing*, 95.

9 Frederick W. Taylor, *The Principles of Scientific Management* (New York: Harper & Brothers, 1911).

10 Geneen and Moscow, *Managing*, 40–42.

11 Thomas Petzinger Jr., *Hard Landing* (New York: Random House, 1995).

12 "Beta Sigma Phi," Wikimedia Foundation, accessed July 15, 2019, https://en.wikipedia.org/w/index.php?title=Beta_Sigma_Phi&oldid=906443180.

13 James P. Armatas, "The Conforming Role of Successful Food Service Workers," *Journal of Counseling Psychology* 10, no. 3, VA Center, Wadsworth, Kansas (Fall 1963).

14 Donald E. Lundberg and James P. Armatas, *The Management of People in Hotels, Restaurants, and Clubs*, Fourth Edition (Dubuque: Wm. C. Brown, 1974).

15 Drucker, "Business Objectives and Survival Needs."

16 Frederick W. Taylor, *The Principles of Scientific Management* (New York: Harper & Brothers, 1911). See also: Frederick W. Taylor, *The Principles of Scientific Management* (Miami: Miami University, 2008).

17 Elton Mayo, *The Human Problems of an Industrial Civilization* (Cambridge: Harvard University Press, 1933).

18 Carl R. Rogers, *Client-Centered Therapy* (London: Constable & Robinson, 1953).

19 Abraham H. Maslow, *Motivation and Personality* (Homewood: Dorsey, 1954).

20 Frederick I. Herzberg, *The Motivation to Work* (New York: John Wiley & Sons, 1966).

21 Douglas T. McGregor, *The Human Side of Enterprise* (New York: McGraw Hill, 1960).

22 Alfred J. Marrow, *The Practical Theorist* (New York: Basic Books, Inc., 1984).

23 Richard Beckhard, *Organizational Development: Strategies and Models* (Reading, MA: Addison-Wesley Publishing Company, 1969).

24 Peter F. Drucker, *The Practice of Management* (New York: HarperCollins Publishers, 1954).

9 781734 641424